A Universal Learning Manual

Many have stated that the **Knowing the Real You** portion of this book could be called the **Recipe of Life** while the **Virtues Knowledge** contains the Ingredients to the recipe of the richness of life. This recipe must be ingested to become a part of one's being, a true part of our intellect and soul; a most important part of understanding how we actually function emotionally and spiritually!

The Wonderful World of Knowledge©

KNOWING THE REAL YOU

Second Edition

Copyright 1998 by Donald C. Decker

Library of Congress Cataloging in Publication Data

All rights reserved. No part of this book may be reproduced or transmitted in any form or by any means. No recording or information storage or retrieval system may be used without written permission from the author/publisher. Basic Western Book Company.

ISBN# 0 - 9649790 - 1 – 2

Get out of your box! Set yourself free to reality and truth! For the sake of the real you cause a transformation from religious tradition to the greatness of: Spiritual Sacredness!!

Today our wonderful religions have nearly abandoned the sacredness of humanity for exclusive conquest! This is not acceptable!

In the lessons herein you will learn many things!

A wise man changes his mind – a fool never will. Be of those who search for Truth.

Challenge your delusions of what you think you know and who you think you are!

Rise above the vengeful, the vulgar and the vain.

Conquer your compulsion towards apathy, grief, fear and anger.

Banish envy, greed and gorging from the sanctity of your soul.

Abandon your pettiness, justifications and judgments all for your sake and the world around you! Enjoy the wonderments of your life!

Get in Touch with the deepest and highest feeling in your heart!

Make a vow of self-control and assertiveness.

Wake up to the true purpose of your life.

Resolve to walk steadfast in your own truth.

Hold true to your highest dreams!

Become radiantly full of life.

Love yourself and others constantly.

Discover the Great Soul!

Give your heart to GOD first.

Live in VIRTUE!

Donald Charles Decker – Author-Publisher-Teacher

KNOWING THE REAL YOU

THE EIGHT LEVELS OF HUMAN CONSCIOUSNESS

PREFACE

We all yearn to know our inner self and our inner spirit. We strive to find true purpose and meaning in our lives. If we succeed, our reward is Universally-given wisdom and knowledge that gives us freedom, a fulfilled life, joy and happiness. This knowledge was known to only a few until recently.

THE EIGHT LEVELS OF HUMAN CONSCIOUSNESS provide us with the psychological and spiritual foundation on a step-by-step basis to learn the reasons of behavior. This book attempts to explain the essence of our human spirit. It will assist in the journey to reach the higher levels of human consciousness and as a result, discover the true reason for our existence.

My purpose in writing this book is to assist those seekers to achieve a more in-depth understanding of themselves. I hope the reader will study this work as an important text for the betterment of their life and of all that surrounds them. The words and practices in this book are essential to your life's progress. Understand CONSCIOUSNESS!

Knowing the Real You can help take down the obstacles, boundaries, veils and clouds that keep us from our real self — the image of God that dwells in each of us.

Knowing the Real You can bring to reality the enlightenment, joy, peace and happiness that is the real you!

Knowing the Real You can assist the spiritual you, of love, peace, and harmony.

Knowing the Real You can let your light shine and bring about virtuous living.

> "O God! Refresh and gladden my spirit. Purify my heart. Illumine my powers. I lay all my affairs in Thy hand. Thou art my Guide and my Refuge. I will no longer be sorrowful and grieved; I will be a happy and joyful being. O God! I will no longer be full of anxiety, nor will I let trouble harass me. I will not dwell on the unpleasant things of life.
>
> O God! Thou art more friend to me than I am to myself. I dedicate myself to Thee, O Lord." - 'Abdu'l-Baha'

KNOWING THE REAL YOU

THE EIGHT LEVELS OF HUMAN CONSCIOUSNESS

ORIENTATION

Religionists, scientists and psychologists of all ages have pondered the essence of that special creation: **humankind**. However, the truth of mankind's existence and purpose has been understood through the ages by only a few. In this text we will find the process of knowing ourselves. The welfare of the individual is inseparable from the welfare of society as a whole. The world is becoming a smaller place as we can view the world from our living rooms and see for ourselves how the actions of a few can influence and change the lives of many.

Today, the age of enlightenment is at hand. The truth of the essence of humankind can be known by all. But to unlock the mysteries of human consciousness and capabilities, we must seek and know more about our Creator and ourselves.

The Bible states, "God created man in His own image, in the image of God created He him; male and female created He them. And God said unto them, 'Be fruitful, and multiply, and replenish the earth, and subdue it; and have dominion' . . . and so it was."

This tells us our essence truly is in the **Image of God** revealed in all the Holy Books. We received these gifts at the time of conception. **The perfection of Creation is within all of us.**

We were also endowed with reason and free will. We have the choice to reach our highest levels of consciousness or to stay trapped in the lower realms of human existence.

If we will come under the guidance of the True Educator and are rightly trained, we become the spirit of spirits, the center of the divine appearances, the source of spiritual qualities, and the receptacle of divine inspirations. If we are deprived of this education, we can become the manifestation of the lower self, the source of dark and ignorant conditions.

It does not take a church to find our true self. We can seek our true self in whatever form we choose. We can live in peace, harmony and love. We will be able to accept that which comes our way. Or we can turn away from our Creator and live in turmoil, degradation and as some say "hell on earth," as lonely, fearful beings - the result of our lack of understanding as to our true purpose. The choice is ours! We are all capable and important beings! We should all seek the true divine self. With knowledge and understanding we can do it!

Our greatest gift is that of <u>intellect</u> — the ability to <u>understand</u>. Understanding is the power by which we acquire knowledge of all creation and the various stages of our emotional existence. This same intellect allows the understanding of much that is invisible: **A Divinely created spiritual world of which we are a part.**

Intellect is in truth the most precious gift bestowed upon mankind by Divine bounty. Mankind among all created things possesses great intellect. The Creator gave this power to humankind that it might be used for the advancement of the individual and civilization, for the good of all humanity to increase love, harmony and peace.

We should learn to properly think. We can learn by listening, learn by reading, learn by looking, learn by feeling, learn by quiet meditation, learn by spiritual caring; the important thing is to learn and to learn we must THINK! Think in the quiet NOW!

THE FIRST STEP

The first step in learning is found in acceptance, not rejection. Knee-jerk rejection of differing ideas and prejudice stops the process of learning. It stops the brain from taking in good information and keeps one in ignorance. We must be open to the possibility that our present concepts and beliefs may not be based on the whole truth. The purpose for us may have been skewed by those in power throughout history. Society at large rarely teaches these truths of enlightenment. We must perfect our power of discernment.

To begin the process of discernment we must be open to the truths that are all around us. Study the Holy Books without prejudice. There are many Holy Books. Give in to the possibility of fact, though different from your present thinking. It is a part of our natural intellectual progression that we go beyond our present knowledge base and investigate and contemplate other cultures and religions. Using mental and spiritual discernment, we will begin to develop into the person we are intended to be with true understanding.

Beware of the false beliefs based on dogma, ritual and superstition. Know that in all of us are the innate possibilities of demonic to angelic behaviors. There is no hell. There is no devil. They both reside in our own capacity as do the angels of our own self. Guilt is a manmade product for control by certain authorities. It is time to get REAL.

Knowledge is the true empowerment of

personal advancement. Strive to develop a new openness of wider thought, as the world is vast and interesting. Even if we make a great effort to know the world's secrets, we shall never know but a drop in the ocean of knowledge and wisdom. Do not be content with anything less than possessing all the knowledge and discernment you possibly can.

If you are not enjoying the present moments in your life it is because your addictions, desires, attachments, demands, expectations, emotional programming and models of how life should treat you are making you dwell in the past. Are you dwelling on the imagined future preventing you from happiness in the precious present? The addictions and obsessions of living in the realm of lower human consciousness cause traumas of life. Addictions cause mental, emotional and physical pain and suffering. You can recognize when an <u>addiction</u> is in control because your bio-computer (brain) is using <u>emotional programming</u> to make you irritated, angry, jealous, confused, tired, bored, defeated, fearful, resentful or generally upset in one way or another.

These destructive conditions tend to cause a life of unhappiness, ignorance and despair. They are the basic reasons for neglect of friends, relatives and family. At their worst, they cause individuals to take drugs, commit violence, abuse their own children, and even commit murder. Yet, no matter how horrendous our acts may be, we always want to be understood and loved. We must first understand our addictions and how we can begin to free ourselves from them.

Solutions to problems in our life come when we replace negative habits and addictions with positive loving ones. Only then do we tune into the people and things around us. We are able to love everyone unconditionally, even the people we do not know. We "see" all the people and things in the world around us from a calm place deep inside us, where everything we need to understand intuitively wells up within us. We develop insights that yield exactly what we need to do in order to flow with the river of life around us. We receive the greatest gifts of life by our new giving and loving attitudes.

When we reach the higher levels of consciousness, we keep ourselves in a state where we are totally involved and yet totally non-addicted, <u>for it is our involvement that is conditional, not our love</u>. We give each other freedom and unconditional acceptance. We love and serve each other in an ego-less way. When the deepest harmonizing of energies take place between people, we enjoy just being together. We are able to experience a deep inner peace by simply being in each other's presence.

When we create a beautiful, peaceful world

in our surroundings, we also help everyone around us to find the peace and happiness they seek. We realize every person is essential to peace and tranquility on this planet. We begin to realize the problems in the world can be solved when all of the people on earth live in ways characterized by loving and serving others. We know that every feeling we have, every thought and communication we make, can add to the world's loving energy which will propagate itself forever in a chain-reaction.

The positive progress and development of the individual multiplies to the essence of a better world. At this growth point, we recognize our innate responsibilities. In the development of an advancing society no one is excluded from responsibility.

Everyone must learn to freely give and accept love As we learn and define the actual conscious behavior levels and reprogram our addictive emotional programming, we naturally become better people. We must study and recognize the names of the conscious levels. As we go through the understanding of the four lower realms of behavior keep your sights on your growth toward the transforming level of unconditional love.

Some of us may discover we are held in bondage by the emotionally backed demands of the four lower or materialistic behavior levels.

The four lower levels are merely the building blocks to the four higher levels of conscious skills. May you be blessed as you continue your study toward knowing the real you.

- How do we free ourselves so we can reach the higher levels of our being?

- How do we discover our true self?

Learn the Keys that open your doors of progress.

The first step for change or growth is found in freeing ourselves of all addictions. We seek the truth of our possibilities. We do not dwell on our addictive past. We will realize our spiritual powers that peacefully take over our ego-driven power level thought and behaviors. We must replace our painful addictions with spiritually guided preferences.

WE CHANGE ADDICTIONS TO PREFERENCES.

<u>Addictions according to Webster</u>:
Compulsive psychological need - habit forming.

<u>Addictions according to Decker</u>:
Anything that we do not have preference control of.

The capacity and capability of eight very distinct levels of human consciousness influence human behavior. The lower four levels have monopolized the world's behavior since the beginning of recorded history. Mankind both individually and socially has been addicted to the aspects and details of the mundane yet necessary conditions provided by these lower conscious levels. The barbaric acts of man's inhumanities to man have been acted out by the lower four level addictions of:

1. **SURVIVAL**
2. **SECURITY**
3. **SENSATION**
4. **MATERIAL POWER**

It is time in the natural progression of humanity to mature in the higher levels of human consciousness. The whole earth is beginning its ascension to higher consciousness and understanding. This is the greatest of all times in human history. The day of light, enlightenment and knowledge: the day of the beginning of human maturity. Be aware for in the chaos of this time a great enlightenment takes place: The day of knowledge is coming to the human species. The Blessed Beauty said in 1844, <u>"I bring you an ocean of knowledge in the days to come compared to a drop from all times past</u>." The ocean comes faster and faster.

Humankind is leaving behind 6800 years of barbaric adolescent behavior, desperately seeking the human maturity that brings personal and world peace. We are moving toward this virtuous maturity. It will come by an act of will or by a painful catastrophe.

By recognition of the 5th level of consciousness - Agape Love, the driving force in the understanding and action of mature human behavior – we will reflect the love of our Creator in our lives. The greatest catalyst for human progress is love. Give up all else and make love your true power. Then you will have everything you desire.

Mankind is soon to recognize that in every being with Universal love resides a Divine universal energy. This energy produces an inner joy and peace that allows us to feel True Love as we endure life's hardships. As we move into the higher consciousness, a new attitude toward our Creator, our loved ones and the whole of mankind becomes a part of our lives. As we live and feel Agape Love, we nurture also the virtues of love, justice, giving, forgiveness, kindness, and courtesy. As more and more of us exude Agape Love, the essence of human goodness found in the virtues of humankind will bring about a harmonious society.

Caring individuals, local societies and basically the world, must now address the four higher levels of consciousness and understanding. These conscious levels are essential to the maturing of the human species. These levels have always existed for they are a part of the powerful aspects of the human creation divinely designed by an Almighty Creator. However, the conscious recognition by a growing critical mass of people is recent. Now is the time when the divine light of consciousness will begin to fill the hearts of the masses. This is the day of the beginning of human maturity, beyond adolescence. Investigate the image you have of yourself. What kind of impression do you make on others? Is it the image that each person was created equal? Do you project yourself as a virtuous person, an achieving person, a competent person, a loving person, or a caring person? Are you a good mother-husband-sister-brother-father, a business person, an artistic person, or a generous person? Or are you a help-poor-me person, someone that the world takes advantage of, a dropout, a dope addict, an alcoholic? Could you be lazy, lethargic and apathetic, not caring?

Hopefully you are not an angry abuser or a negative influence on the society around you. Or perhaps your ego is guarding your perceived image of your present nature. Does your ego see you as a "pure" climber of the mystical mountain? Do you get upset when someone points out that your way is not the only way or not the best way for he or she? Is your ego directing your energy and your life? Who do you think you are? Generally, you are not who you think you are but what you think.

When you clearly see your various activities, games and personal boundaries as a drama that your ego is trying to guard and enhance, you will understand who you now think you are. However, you are none of these things. You are going through these acts to discover the conscious being that you really are. These acts and activities constantly change in your life. If you grow toward higher consciousness, most of the negatives will be gone in the near future. The more truly meaningful ways remain, but over the span of life they will change. As you progress in consciousness, you will see with a new perspective the way you are busily engaged in the mechanical playing out of roles in which you have programmed yourself. These roles are most often survival, security, sensation and material power ego-driven addictions.

All of these activities keep us trapped to a great degree. They keep us vulnerable and on a roller coaster of pleasure and pain. Most addictive models we are guarding represent patterns of personalities that are a function of the time and place where you were born or grew up. Society and demands of those pressures established our present consciousness. Some were fortunate to have lived in an environment of love, understanding, education, spiritual devotion and material plenty. Some were not. No matter which, it is time to move ahead.

The societies of the past were absolute as to class and social level. In this age, equality surges through the veins of the world. In the emerging New World, the caste system will be leveled. The boundaries of freedom and liberty will enhance all of humankind. The only restriction will come within the individual. The levels of society may be unequal, but the human opportunity will be there for the masses. The world is here for us to enjoy, but we can only do so when we are free from the false roles we play in the drama of life. Human beings with their rational minds enjoy solving problems. We tend to take our problems with such seriousness that we kill the spontaneity and joy of our present life situation. <u>We need a way to discriminate between what we essentially are and the motivational models that generate our behavior. Let's investigate deeper into our real self.</u>

Be not mistaken; the _essence_ of man is not his rational mind! Aristotle missed the mark when he tried to define man as rational. This is the part of our being that has the ability to use language to analyze, calculate, produce thoughts and images, sort out sensations, store memories and retrieve them, use symbols and to compare beliefs and assumptions. Our rational mind is a magnificent "sixth sense" that can help us in our journey to higher consciousness if we know how to use it properly. Or it can keep us helplessly trapped in the four lower levels of consciousness by slavishly cooperating with our ego to form rigid defenses that try to maintain whatever programming we are stuck on now. Let it go! The ego controls in the lower levels; it deceives us! Ego causes false ideas and gives us pain.

If we are not our _social roles_, _our body_, or _our rational mind_, then what is left? Are we _our senses_, the perceivers through which visual, auditory, tactile, taste and olfactory data are received? Or are we _our emotions_, those feelings that we expend so much energy in either getting or avoiding? Are we our programming, the collections of desires, motivations, expectations and demands on which our egos focus most of our attention and energy? Or are we _our ego_, the "master controller", the false idea manufacturer which is an absolute dictator when we are trapped in the lower four levels of consciousness?

Psychologists and many thinkers of the past have laid claim on each of these conditions. <u>Fortunately, the essential part of us is none of these</u>. Our essence is something we experience to help us grow to the highest consciousness. Higher consciousness is not achieved by substance use of any kind. In the truth of unconditional love, we begin to find the peaceful and powerful essence of humankind. <u>The essence of human beings is their conscious awareness. The essence of our being can only be found in our high levels of consciousness</u>. The immediately recognizable parts of this consciousness are found in the innate virtues such as love, honesty, integrity, justice, kindness, caring

To understand what is meant by conscious awareness, look straight ahead and notice the images that are being transmitted through your eyes, then close your eyes. When your visual sensations disappeared and the functions mentioned above shut down, your **conscious awareness** remained. Behind all your thoughts, sensations and images, your conscious awareness is always there. Most of the time we keep it smothered under a ceaseless condition of words, activities, thoughts and sensations which keep our minds analyzing, calculating, symbolizing, talking and remembering.

It is written, "Be still and know that I am God." **Go to a Quiet Place**. We only experience our essence fully when we have quieted our emotion-backed drama and the torrent of addictive junk churned out by our rational mind.

In the soul of humankind we find our essence, the awareness of consciousness. We are the consciousness that "sees" what is happening on the screen of life. In this level, we can observe from a quiet corner of our being. We are free. Our essence is becoming pure conscious awareness, free from our addictions and the bondage of self. We learn to accept. We become spiritually aware human beings. We gain Universal Knowledge and health.

The simple names of these four highest levels of consciousness are: **UNCONDITIONAL LOVE - CONSCIOUS REALITY - CONSCIOUS AWARENESS - UNIVERSAL CONSCIOUSNESS.** These names may not be as familiar to you as the lower four levels because they have not been a part of the common knowledge of humankind until recently.

Each year contains 31,536,000 seconds. Each second offers us an opportunity to grow toward a new and vital consciousness. How we and those around us benefit from this time is the responsibility of each of us. Time is of the essence. It is not to be wasted. Some time should be used for growth, learning, and peaceful cooperation.

If the peoples of the world are to gain their true destiny and advance toward the spirit of True Creation they must understand the following particular processes and behaviors caused by the knowledge within these conscious levels. **The essence of this understanding is no less than individual to global interconnected peace processes. The Universe and everything in it are interconnected, any separation is a negative influence against us; we are all connected. Prejudice is always a separation from truth.**

To find our answers we must understand some basic aspects of the human creation itself. <u>Humankind, from the time of birth, undergoes changes attributed to their environment and experience, in levels of consciousness, degrees of intellect, emotional stability and spiritual awareness</u>.

In animals we find a relatively fixed lifestyle based on survival instinct and need. Human activity and behavior shifts along a much broader spectrum of awareness depending on the "conscious level" reached. To reach our potential with the higher levels of spiritual consciousness, we must go through a cleansing. Empty yourself of old junk. Let your mind be at peace; give it a rest. Practice stillness!

Then open your mind to spiritual thought, virtues, etc. Universal energy will come to you.

Open mind — open heart. With an open heart and mind you will become honestly noble to meet the essence of your individual calling.

Start the thinking process of discernment and detachment.

GET RID OF THE MEANINGLESS JUNK!

Go to next page and begin your studies.

YOU

I believe in the way you are for the you came there through what you see.
Though I most admire the way you will be.

If you should ever doubt your dreams in any way.
I know you will have a better day.

If you worry don't worry too long.
For you will find your place in the world in which you belong.

I know you will get where you're going some day.
For what ever happens you will find a way.

I hope the lessons you study in this book
Will get you there without a second look!

LOWER HUMAN CONSCIOUSNESS

In lower human consciousness, we are ego-driven, subject-object oriented and driven by **survival, security, sensation** and **material power** needs. We increasingly operate from the rational mind which makes us inflexible and self-centered. We guard and protect our habitual addictions and personal behavior patterns, no matter if they destroy us. Any addiction limits our growth and disturbs our peace. We keep ourselves in lower consciousness levels by concentrating on images we have of ourselves, what we did in the past, what the world was like in the past, or what we plan in the future.

It is best not to hang on to discussing the past or to let our consciousness dwell on the past because it keeps us from fully experiencing the present moment in our life. Nor is it best to be constantly preoccupied with thoughts of the future. If there is something we need to do right now, then we should get busy and do it. Living in the past or worrying about the future only takes away from the eternally precious present.

Low conscious level living produces negative physical health. All of the lower levels are material in nature and keep us in the prison of self. This program of conscious awareness development will release us from that selfish condition where we perform in the four lower levels. Holding on to these addictions allows

stress to become part of our daily lives. Stress eventually produces physical health problems. Most addictions and stress will kill us prematurely. They also greatly diminish our quality of life.

The lowest potential of these levels produces the world's thieves, murderers, dictators and psychotic abusers. It is where we get all kinds of control freaks and chauvinistic behaviors. It is where unhealthy co-dependence dwells. In the higher levels you will find the power of detachment from these negative aspects of life.

Lower level addiction manifests itself in the satanic, hurtful, cruel, cold, indifferent, insensitive, irresponsible, egocentric and arrogant, negative behavior. It condemns a person, a family, a nation or any organization or institution to a high cost dysfunction or demise. <u>America's prison, crime and dropout statistics give us an insight on this truth</u>. The world of hate and prejudice resides here.

In America today we have a high percentage of our population residing in the higher levels of consciousness and behavior. However, it appears that many are holding on to their lower level addictions. If we do not help change the course of individuals toward sensitive behaviors of the upper levels, we will continue to contribute to the destruction of our own society.

In the lower level behaviors we stay 'blind and deaf' to ignorance and insensitivity. We choose to ignore reality, not only in our immediate surroundings but we continue to be blind as to public and government activities. We tend to remain silent when abuses prevail. The addiction of the four lower levels is dangerous to our own beings, our families and our society at large. An ego-driven person is basically blind and deaf of their true spirit. We destroy ourselves and people around us when we follow the dictates of our ego. In order to grow and rise to our wonderful spiritual and intellectual self, we must subdue our ego.

First, we must understand that ego, as powerful as it is, has no form. Today we have a more precise analysis of what ego is. Ego is an invisible formless mental idea of self. Ego tends to control our false self-image by programming our outside world while denouncing our inner spiritual self. Thus, the outer illusion becomes your perceived self and takes over your behavior, which is based on lower level activity.

Your higher, real self is denied for you have allowed this idea the ego has developed and controlled to become you. Ego is your false self. It builds walls between you and your true self. It destroys your real self and your potential. The ego is the opposite of your true self. Ego destroys harmony and brings separation. <u>Ego denies Universal Love.</u> Your ego-driven self could allow you to believe you are better than other people. It can allow you to develop hate, prejudice and fear. This condition denies us reaching the 5th level of unconditional love, a major step in our maturity of true self. We must detach ourselves from self-absorption and ego-driven imaging and behavior if we are to be truly free to grow and recognize our true gracious self. Real personal freedom comes when we free ourselves from the power of ego. We start to learn balance. Life becomes a positive experience!

LET IT GO AND ENJOY LIFE!

THE CONSCIOUSNESS OF UNCONDITIONAL LOVE IS POSITIVE FOR ALL. IT HAS NO NEGATIVES; IT ONLY HELPS. IT HINDERS NO ONE; IT STRENGTHENS ALL. IT IS THE VERY FOUNDATION OF PEACE AND HAPPINESS FOR INDIVIDUALS, FAMILIES AND SOCIETY AT LARGE. TRUE HAPPINESS OCCURS ONLY WHEN OUR CONSCIOUSNESS IS NOT DOMINATED BY OLD ADDITIONS OR EGO DEMANDS AND WE ARE ABLE TO EXPERIENCE LIFE AS A SERIES OF PREFERENCES. THIS IS FREEDOM!

YOU ARE A PRECIOUS BEING: BELIEVE IT!

HIGHER HUMAN CONSCIOUSNESS

In higher human consciousness, wide-ranging insight and deep intuitive understanding giving us full flexibility to flow in mutually supportive and loving ways have replaced ego-driven negative emotions. We transcend beyond inflexible habits or personal patterns. We always endeavor to expand our love, consciousness and loving compassion by experiencing everything that everyone else does or says as though we had experienced or said it ourselves. However we constantly use the power of discernment to only allow the good to come into our psychic. Love diminishes ego! Love diminishes fear! Love creates harmony and peaceful co-existence. Love is the power and connector of the universe. Love powers true spirituality! Love diminishes ego and arrogance!

In our spiritual world, the divine attributes are innate. In that realm there is neither separation nor disintegration that characterize the world of material existence. Spiritual existence for all of us is absolute immortality, completeness and unchangeable, positive being. We must be thankful that the Universe has created for us both material blessings and spiritual attributes. We have material gifts and spiritual graces, the outer sight to view the lights of Universal splendor and the inner vision by which we may perceive the glory of life.

We must strive with all the energies of heart, soul and mind to develop and manifest the excellence of the Virtue's, latent within the realities of the phenomenal human being.

The human essence may be compared to a tiny seed. If we sow the seed, a mighty tree appears from it. The virtues of the seed are revealed in the tree; it puts forth branches, leaves, and blossoms which produce fruit. All these virtues were hidden and were potential in the seed. Through the blessings and bounty of the cultivation of virtues, the reality of human kind becomes apparent. Similarly, the merciful God, our creator, has deposited within human reality virtues that are somewhat latent at this time but have glorious potential. Through education and culture these virtues deposited by a loving God will become apparent in the human reality even as the growth of a tree emanates from a germinating seed. Universal Energy will come to you.

The combination of the spirit of man and the Divine Spirit is so powerful within the human being that it is incalculable. This amazing power is a distinctive attribute of the human being and resides in no other kingdoms of the universe. The great gifts of intelligence and understanding allow the human species to ascend to a spiritual empowerment on this earth that is harmonious with the universe and can provide a euphoric, joyful life.

Why would any sane human being want to deny themselves the innate virtues that can cause immediate ascension to a high and productive, harmonious place in life? Material advancement has been evident in the world for many years, but there is now a need of spiritual advancement in like proportion. We must strive unceasingly to accomplish the development of the spiritual nature in man, and endeavor with tireless energy to advance humanity toward the nobility of its true and intended station. Each of us must recognize that it is time to come out of the addictions of the four lower levels of materialistic life and ascend and recognize the spiritual consciousness available.

The spiritual aspect of our being must now be the focus and focal point of our study. Daily activities empowered by the simple universal virtue given each of us will enhance our lives. Spirituality and the knowledge of it are essential to our growth. For the body of mankind is accidental; it is of little importance. The time of its disintegration will inevitably come. But the spirit of man is essential and eternal. It is a divine bounty. The spiritual reality is, therefore, of greater importance than the physical body. Let us humble ourselves and eradicate ego-driven addictions.

When our ego has less and less work to do as the slave of our addictions, we begin to experience the whole spectrum of the present.

We no longer exist in the pain of the past, or in the vague future. Our perception increases enormously. We have a higher predictability of our thinking and actions. We can accept help without feeling that an obligation is created because we are mature "receivers". <u>We begin to "see" with our inner spiritual eye first and then our biological eyes</u>.

When we live in the upper levels of consciousness, we find we are blessed with better physical and mental health. We begin to flow and our countenance shines. Our circulatory system opens and positively affects our brain and organs to make them function better. Colds or illness become rare. We constantly undergo spiritual cleansing. We must strive daily for higher conscious skills described in the four spiritual levels.

To reach higher human consciousness, we must strive to reprogram our bio-computer that produces our thoughts and actions. The negative traits of our being must be replaced by the positive conditions of love and respect for all of our fellow kind. Each person should realize and say:

> "I PERCEIVE EVERYONE, INCLUDING MYSELF, AS AN AWAKENED BEING WHO IS HERE TO CLAIM HIS OR HER BIRTHRIGHT TO THE HIGHER CONSCIOUSNESS PLANES OF UNCONDITIONAL LOVE AND ONENESS."

When we reach the higher human consciousness, eventually, no matter what happens, we experience everything as love. We finally arrive at the place where nothing that happens in the world around us knocks out our consciousness of loving. We can emotionally accept everything. Our intellect may question an act, so we develop emotional stability merely by ascending to a higher consciousness of unconditional love. We can always return love no matter what a person says or does. And by doing this, <u>we help others transcend their negative addictions</u>. If we remain loving and understanding even when others try to hurt us, they may become disarmed and begin to find that capacity to love in themselves. **Everything is either an effective or ineffective way of creating love, peace and oneness.**

The bio-computer with which we are equipped is the most remarkable instrument created in the universe. Our goal is to learn to use it properly. It has tremendous capabilities in visual and auditory inputs and outputs every moment of our life. It operates with enormous power primarily on sub-conscious levels, with only a small portion of its activity operating at the conscious level. Our advancement into the higher levels is a matter of learning how to properly use our exquisite mechanism. The bio-computer is always under-going change. Let's program virtuous spiritual imaging, which will absolutely defeat our cowardly ego.

When we really learn to operate our bio-computer, we will be able to fully realize our potential for a full and happy life. Understanding the eight levels of human consciousness and learning to live each day in the fifth, sixth, seventh and eighth levels is an important key to finding true happiness and meaning in our lives. This process of reprogramming can be achieved by anyone. This knowledge can be brought into the life of all human beings. **WE CAN ALL LEARN TO LOVE**, it is just a matter of time. I would wholly recommend that you diligently work for its maturing in your own life. Universal Energy will be a constant *for you!*

LOVE IS PATIENT, LOVE IS KIND. IT DOES NOT ENVY, IT IS NOT RUDE, AND IT IS NOT ANGERED. IT KEEPS NO RECORD OF WRONGS, ETC. THE BIBLE

LOVE NEVER FAILS!!

- Remember love is the answer! Let your light shine!

- People need love always, especially when they don't deserve it.

- We are never more discontented with others than when we are discontented with ourselves - do not criticize; **love.**

- Let us not get lost in the "dailyness" of life.

- Let go of prejudice! IN your soul is only love. Know it! Go There!

- Our voluntary thoughts not only reveal what we think we are, they predict what we will become.

- Be cautious of your thoughts! Make them all positive! They are your future!

- Do not abuse the power of thought. Make it positive.

- Practice defeating ego - you'll love it! Humbleness is a VIRTUE!

As we will soon learn, in the EIGHT LEVELS OF HUMAN CONSCIOUSNESS the personally empowering transformation toward a place of total capability is simply the ability to love unconditionally. This enables the human being to be all they can be in the realms of life's fulfillment. One of the major rewards by accomplishing your fullness represented in these conscious levels is a life of peace and tranquility. The road towards these accomplishments is paved with positive thought processes. Do not get involved with misuse of your mind. Keep it clean, caring and advancing. Concentrate on the virtues of life. Be discerning in the quiet of the now!

Rid yourself of all the offenses you have committed. Forgive yourself and others of the offenses committed throughout your life – FORGIVE! You will then have a new heart and a new spirit.

The higher levels of consciousness described in this text actually produces a radiant and victorious spirit. As we study and work the text, we must keep in mind that "our life is what our thoughts make it". Yes, if we think happy thoughts, we will be happy. If we think miserable thoughts, we will be miserable. If we think fearful thoughts, we will be fearful. If we think failure, we will certainly fail. If we wallow in self-pity, people will shun us and avoid us. **I believe that you are not what you think you are; but a being beyond your thought.** dcd

As we have already found out in the dramas of our past, thought leads to attitude and together they become our future. It is imperative that we immediately cut off any negative imaging that could become an addiction. Addictions have the capacity to stop the growing of the intellectual and spiritual enthusiasm that gives us life.

THINK PEACE! THINK LOVE!

Peace, peace, wonderful peace,
Flowing from the loving Father,
Sweep over my spirit forever I pray
In fathomless billows of love.

GOALS OF THIS COURSE

- The great Creator and the creation first!
- Learn to Love.
- No more self-deception.
- No more ego-driven self judgment.
- Constantly seek truth.
- Healthy self-love recognizing the true you.
- Personal freedom from all addictions.
- Seek Wisdom, Knowledge & Understanding.
- Always control ego.
- Learn the power of giving and serving.
- Recognize the real you - the God within.
- Harmonious successful lifestyles.
- No more doubts, No more fears, No more conflicts, No more worrying, No more confrontation, Just Peace and the excitement of growth.
- Learn to connect your mind/spirit with the Divine mind/spirit for perfect peace. Quiet your inner self. Be still and know real peace.
- Subdue ego, gain health, happiness, & peace.
- Release guilt — forgive yourself and others.

BEGIN

This first level makes us preoccupied and at times paranoid about food, clothing, shelter, or whatever we equate with personal survival.

SURVIVAL

Survival is the first or lowest level of human consciousness. It lacks spiritual content. Survival usually dictates behavior patterns of desperation and worry. It causes stress, distress and in this day can be damaging to one's physical, mental and spiritual health.

Until this radiant century, humankind has toiled hard and known few conveniences, exhausting energy for survival, security and the necessities of existence. Food, clothing and shelter were difficult and hard to come by. Man had to hunt daily for the means of survival and his enemies were many. Emotional alarms were needed to command full attention to danger and survival. Early man was programmed for automatic duality - automatic feelings of oneness at one extreme, and threat and paranoia at the other. Survival required instant domination of consciousness to meet the perils of a wild and dangerous environment. Survival of the fittest by fight and flight has been the defense and offense of mankind since those crude times.

In the first level of consciousness, our bio-computers are still programmed, to a large degree, for fight or flight, a fast release of adrenaline, a rapid heartbeat and automatic anger and fear. In our social interactions, our mind and conscious-ness magnify molehills into mountains and this constant distortion destroys our energy, insight, and true progress and ability to love and care for others. Survival attitudes develop ego-fear factors. These tend to distort our recognition of our true self.

Paranoid dualistic individuals who cannot love themselves or others become accident-prone and tend to get heart trouble, ulcers and other psychosomatic caused diseases. They can be triggered into violence for seemingly little or no provocation. To be held in this level of consciousness is the pity of our times. It takes understanding, special education, concern and caring to help these souls. Survival of the fittest and an "eye for an eye" are both laws and conditions rebuked many centuries ago. Love, understanding and empathy are the demand of this day.

The thoughts and attitudes of survival thinking develop daily addictions of low result materialism and pushes out our spiritual light. Little or no progress toward higher achievement can be accomplished under this addiction that produces low self-esteem. The persons addicted to these lower levels of consciousness will never be whole. The ignorance and ridiculous demands of these lower levels have caused the destructive and historical regression of the civilizations of the world. Survival thinking is the lowest ego-driven behavior, which destroys people, nations and whole civilizations.

When we learn to cut through our paranoid programming we are on our way to higher consciousness and a fuller and happier life. We must recognize this, before it can be brought into the focus of truth and solved. The old struggle for survival keeps us blind to the realities of opportunities that are constantly available. Survival attitudes are exactly the addicted emotional programming that keeps us in poverty for we cannot see the possibilities that are all around us. Our languages, the words we use, are usually negative and demeaning. This level produces the lowest behaviors in our society. Survival thinking produces low self-esteem. It produces a no-love environment, which in turn produces violent behavior.

To reduce the murders, rapes, robberies and crimes against the innocent of society, the basic principals of human consciousness must be taught to the masses. We have an obligation to recognize the reality of human advancement and to teach it. Survival is a necessity to life; however, it no longer can be an addiction or animalistic instinct. The caveman era has long past. Most of us understand survival in this day is just basically going to work. It is really a part of our human past therefore we will not dwell on it in this text. However, we should know the lower level behaviors contribute greatly to the cost of society, from human suffering to the economic cost of war, welfare, prison systems, etc.

This primitive aspect of man has changed in the millennium of "recent" times. It was long ago when our ancestors built the first cities. As civilization grew, survival depended less and less on the need for instant fight or flight from danger. Over time, survival became dependent on the ability to tune into one's overall situation, including the surrounding environment. Humankind's survival responses evolved from a pattern of animalistic instincts to ego mechanisms, backed by hair-trigger emotions to develop the next three levels of consciousness: **SECURITY, SENSATION, AND MATERIAL POWER.**

We should not be threatened with survival fears. Today, survival does not depend so much on outside influence. Survival depends on your inner self. The confidence of your true self and spiritual strength guarantees survival. In this state little if any Positive Universal Energy is found in us. Let's depart from survival and move up the consciousness ladder to attain our better position for growth and wholeness.

> **OUR PERSONAL DEVELOPMENT INTO FULFILLING, HAPPY LIVES BEYOND SURVIVAL CONSCIOUSNESS, DEPENDS ON OUR GETTING <u>FREE</u> OF OUR EGO-BACKED, SUBJECT-OBJECT, ME-THEM <u>SECURITY</u>, <u>SENSATION</u>, <u>POWER</u> HANGUPS. SURVIVAL IN MOST OF THE WORLD IS PRESENTLY A REALITY. IT IS TIME TO MOVE ON TO OUR MATURITY SO THAT WE CAN REACH BACK TO HELP OTHER.**

We must begin our rejection of an overpowering ego and demand a balanced, healthy lifestyle by recognizing and developing Virtues thinking. This changing of attitudes usually takes time and a lot of direct effort on our part. We can struggle to learn to reprogram ourselves by a concerted act of volition and spiritual will. We can transform our perceived, ego-driven, false self to our higher self quickly. We are all qualified to recognize the spiritual truth and power within our present being. Rise up out of survival attitudes toward a progressive realization of your true self—you can do it. Let's move up!

SECURITY

Security is the second level of consciousness. This level, in its non-addictive, healthy state, can be driven by concern for self and family. However, when ego-driven, it is addictive. Cars, jewelry and toys of several varieties represent status symbols that give us a false sense of security. Basically, we are stuck in a level of material bondage. This programming forces our consciousness to be dominated by our continuous battle to get "enough" from the world in order to feel secure. This is never real security.

Addiction to this lower consciousness level keeps us from growing to a condition of confidence that would make security easier. We are in fact fighting ourselves again in the false belief that we are some kind of limited being. The truth is that we are already capable of developing a secure life if in fact we will move ahead towards the higher conscious levels. Real self confidence is found in spiritual maturity!

Today, most people are in bondage by heavy debt that is motivated by a corrupt debt system of credit cards and over-spending by individuals and families. We strive for material security when, in fact, trying to keep up with our society takes away real security.

What is it that makes us feel secure?

What is it that makes us feel insecure?

Security is really a sense of confidence & Spiritual Maturity.

One person may feel secure with practically no money at all. Another may feel insecure with a million dollars in the bank. The security center or level of our being automatically triggers feelings of fear and anxiety when the outside world does not conform to our security program.

Observe how much of our time is involved in the unpleasant striving to achieve the conditions that we tell ourselves we must have to feel secure. Yet it is impossible to get enough of whatever it is that we equate with security. We are like the rat that is running as fast as he can in a revolving cartwheel cage. There is no way to get there by running faster or by achieving more efficiently. We escape being trapped in this second level of consciousness when we begin to understand that our flow into higher levels offers you far more security than your lower consciousness struggle for "security" can provide.

Real security only lies in the love you discover through higher consciousness. Even the material aspects of this modern world such as home, autos, finances come with greater ease when the higher conscious levels are achieved. When we are addicted to these lower levels, accomplishments and necessities come to us in a most difficult manner. The lower levels of survival and security represent a struggle that takes our energy and produces very little.

In general, there is nothing about any level of consciousness that is especially right or wrong, good or bad, pure or evil. The key is to recognize and reprogram from this security fear addiction to a true preference commitment to rely on the truth that our survival and security are already provided by an Almighty Creator. Then our growth will depend on completely accepting ourselves and others as we are today, not in some future time when we have conquered our past addictions. Go from here.

> **WE SHOULD ACCEPT WHERE WE ARE BY REALIZING WE ARE EXPERIENCING PERSONAL ADDITIONS OF GROWTH AND KNOWLEDGE THAT GIVE US THE FEELINGS WE NEED FOR OUR NEXT STEP. BY JOYOUSLY USING OUR PRESENT CONDITION AS A STEPPING STONE, OUR GROWTH WILL OCCUR IN THE FASTEST WAY POSSIBLE.**

When we are addicted to developing security or more accurately perceived security, we are giving up to a great degree the goodness, truth and beauty of the world. We are really fighting against ourselves in the development of real security; the absolute inner peace guaranteed in the higher conscious levels. Security in the real sense is not about stocks and bonds, real estate or other investments. However, all of these material security aspects can and will be achieved with less effort by a well managed higher consciousness.

Let us move on for if we dwell on the lower levels they will take away our energy to concentrate and learn the resolution to lower level thinking.

Security becomes a natural, comfortable and simple spiritual lifestyle when we ascend to the four highest levels. Remember that addictive thinking violates the principles of your true, higher self. Let's develop preference thinking based on virtues, values, principles and morality. When we live with higher level thoughts and actions, we are better organized and have wisely taken care of our security factors. Security is not found in these materialistic levels of consciousness, but can be found in the spiritually empowered higher levels.

<u>Let's move up to sensation consciousness.</u>

SENSATION

Sensation is the third level of consciousness. This level is concerned with finding happiness and fulfillment in life by providing ourselves with more and better pleasurable sensations and activities. For many people, sex, drugs and alcohol are the most appealing of all sensations. Other addictive sensations may include music, food, hunting, playing games, becoming a couch potato, hate, money, prejudice or sports. No addiction for the sake of sensation in any level is acceptable to a growing, achieving individual. We must attain and keep flexibility.

People hung up on security consciousness tell themselves "we can be happy if we can feel secure, get more stuff." However, once they begin to feel secure, they find this is not quite true. Instead, they move to the third level and become fixed on manipulating the people and things in their life to provide a constantly varied pattern of sensations to find their happiness. These people still feel an emptiness in their inner self. Most sensation is short lived. Some kinds of sensation are all right. Real security and sensation is a spiritual condition.

A lower level person tries to find answers outside – a higher level person knows the answers are in the egoless/non-addicted/spiritual inside. We can all get there!

For many people, sex is the most sought after sensation. Our lifestyle is designed to provide us with sexual sensation. The people we choose to be with, the clothes we buy, the home we live in and our style of speech, thinking and action is based on our desire to appeal to sexual partners. This is known as subject-object sex, in which we are the subject and others in our lives are sexual objects. There are many problems that come from this fixation. Most importantly, we are operating on a level of consciousness that can never provide real happiness. **We soon realize that all fulfilled relationships must be spiritual, intellectual and physical, in that order.**

Behind the exquisite sexual dance, both parties feel the shallowness of the subject-object relationship. We know something is wrong, even if we don't know exactly what it is. No matter how much sex there is, it is never enough. Many times it is degrading to both parties. It causes grave conflicts in many lives and distrust in many relationships. We are tuning into only a small part of ourselves and an even smaller part of others. Life seems hollow because this third level of consciousness can produce only flashes of pleasure and long periods of indifference and boredom. We become driven, thwarted and not in tune with the "present" flow of life when we are chasing sensation after sensation. Sex, as an act of the physical expression of true love, is wonderful when it has a spiritually loving foundation. Love is the essence of life. Lust is wrong and hurtful.

For others, the path to feeling good is sought through the dangerous sensation of drugs and alcohol. The social acceptance of the use of contrived sensations to find happiness has caused many people to seek these dangerous, demeaning and debilitating substances. Instead of bringing happiness, they disable us from positive advance-ment, destroy our productivity, reduce our physical and mental health, cause serious family problems and can destroy a society. The degradation caused by drugs and alcohol has inflicted more suffering, humiliation, premature death, emotional violence and economic waste than all aspects of humankind except war. **God said, "I created thee noble, why do you debase yourself."** When we are addicted to the four lower levels of human behavior we not only destroy everything around us we eventually destroy ourselves.

The constant search for happiness through sensation whether by food, materialistic possessions, alcohol or drugs keeps us busy, but they are never enough until **we are enough**. Until we find our true spiritual being nothing works.

When we see ourselves as whole through higher personal and spiritual consciousness everything can be enjoyed as part of the great drama of our life. Until then, nothing ever quite does it for us, and the enjoyment we seek will tend to elude us as long as we addictively demand it. When we "upgrade" addictions into positive preferences, we enjoy it all. Sensation for the sake of sensation is the sign of addictive behavior in itself. Sensation by spiritual conscious choice is the beginning of preference wisdom. The actual preference to improve is essential. Let's develop the enthusiasm to go for it! (En-thus-ism: In-God's-power.) Inner commitment to excellence is realized through virtues. Virtues are the tools of excellence in all positive aspects of life. Virtues are the building blocks of your higher destiny.

When we advance to higher levels of consciousness and understanding and develop the capacity for unconditional love, sensations can add to our happiness and well-being as part of a positive flow of our life. Only healthy sensations can contribute to our wellness. When our consciousness is directed primarily toward providing us with the sensation patterns to which we are addicted, we have more energy than when we were hung up on the **security** level. We usually are with people more and need to sleep less. Although the search for happiness through sensation is an improvement over the search for happiness from the **security** level, wisdom, peace and serenity are not yet in sight. When we are trapped in any of these lower aspects of consciousness we experience turmoil, confusion and a desperately shallow existence. We are virtually trapped in the lower realms of human possibility. We miss LIFE!

> **THE WAY TO FREEDOM AND FULFILLMENT IS CERTAIN ONCE WE REALIZE THE TRUE NATURE OF OUR GOD-GIVEN CHARACTER AND UNDERSTAND THE REALMS OF CONSCIOUSNESS. WITH THIS KNOWLEDGE, WE REALIZE EVERYONE HAS THE ABILITY TO ACHIEVE FULFILLMENT, PEACE AND WISDOM. GET OUT OF THE PRISON OF SELF — EXCHANGE THE EGO FOR LOVE AND COURTESY.**

Sensation is essential in the practical senses of hearing, feeling, tasting, smelling and seeing, but they do not of their own condition create special wholeness in people. These senses have to do with bodily functions rather than the matter of spirit or soul. These are base aspects of the human being - which is similar to animals. The human has been given the great gifts of understanding and thought processing. You create your thoughts, which create your intentions, which finally create your reality. Let us discover how we move up to higher function through higher consciousness using free thought without ego contamination. The next level and the last of the lower four levels, Is _Material Power_, still ego-driven to a large degree.

Before we advance remember: To each of us a life is given and with it an awesome and priceless responsibility – the freedom to choose how we live in the world and what we make of ourselves.

You do not have control over all that happens to you, but you do have control over how you respond and what you think, say and do. You are in charge. Where you put your attention, what action you take, is up to you!

The knowledge in this book is personally about you! Believe it!

The time is now. We must seize the moment to change the world around us. To achieve peace and harmony we must change ourselves.

<u>We must discover our great soul</u>.

Material power is mostly the cause of the destruction of humankind. It is an ego–driven hunt for false security and develops arrogance.

As we advance in the course of higher consciousness we will know a lot more about the largest and everlasting part of our being – our great eternal soul. Only in the four higher human conscious levels can we feel and know our own souls health and maturity.

Let us study the last of the lower levels of human existence: Material Power.

MATERIAL POWER

Material Power is the fourth level of consciousness. When our consciousness is focused on this power level, we are greatly concerned with dominating people and situations and with increasing our prestige, wealth and pride. When we become programmed to the degree of obsession in this level, we are doomed to a fall that is usually permanent. The dictators and tyrants of the world fit into this level. With material power, greed destruction soon occurs.

In the extreme, this level is the downfall of humankind. It prevents true progress in the development of a proper and acceptable world order. This level of power consciousness also manifests itself in hundreds of more subtle forms of hierarchy, manipulation and control. It is an ego-driven false imaging condition in which we believe we are our possessions. Our fall comes when these possessions are protected and worshiped more than God.

This power level is the last or fourth level of human consciousness that can never provide us with "enough". As yet, most of the people in the world are still addicted to the four lower levels of survival, security, sensation and material power. The attempt to find happiness through the material power level is a step forward in growth toward higher consciousness. When we are operating from this level, we will have more energy and will interact with more people. However, these are subject-object interactions in which people either cooperate with our power games or they threaten them. In this realm, life is a series of competitive moves and countermoves. When we approach life with obsessive power addictions, we will be instantly resisted by the power addictions of other people. Instead of opening themselves to help us, they close themselves and are automatically antagonistic to our power thrusts, which threaten them. This realm of behavior is typified by win-loose power addictions. We now know that life in a mature sense can be win-win. Everyone is considered in cooperative win-win conditions.

The old addictive process that causes conflict and a competitive win-lose attitude is not acceptable to a mature higher level person. As we progress into the behaviors of the higher conscious levels, we will see very clearly the ingredients of conflict resolution and win-win results.

<u>Are you addicted to this power level of consciousness?</u>

Do you strive for money as a method of wielding power rather than money as a form of security? Do you seek prestige because you think the more of it you have, the more you can manipulate people? Do your power addictions keep you preoccupied with external symbols such as cars, attractive homes, fashionable clothes, etc.? The most dangerous aspect of the power level is to covet or worship your material possessions. Or have you up-leveled the game to "internal" status symbols such as wisdom, knowledge and the spiritual powers of caring, kindness, consideration? Do others perceive you as an interesting, achieving person? Remember; the goals of achievement can be satisfying and healthy. Only when they come near to being an addictive obsession will they become harmful to your very being.

Many times, the more successful a person becomes on the outside, the less successful he or she is on the inside. Typically, the person's energies have been expended for selfish and lower level conscious activities. Anxieties, ulcers and heart disease tend to increase with external "success". We tend to "worry" ourselves, which allows disease and ailments to come in to our being while "protecting" our material world. We destroy real integrity. Whenever you violate or compromise your integrity, there is a great force or power of retribution that will not allow you to go forward.

External success can be properly achieved with a balance of higher level conscious activities and spiritually productive life cultures.

To the degree that our consciousness is based on the lower four levels, we are trapped in many negative aspects of life and human endeavor. We are ready for our next step toward higher consciousness. Only when we deeply realize the utter futility of trying to make it in life using lower consciousness levels can we rise to higher consciousness. This does not necessarily mean we must drastically change our external activities or disperse of our material positions. In fact, the Almighty One who created the universe has prescribed a goodly bounty for all of His children. What we must denounce are our addictive demands and habitual behaviors. Remember: higher ego-less levels allow us to see the real self; one of giving, caring and compassion.

We soon learn certain acts against self and family must be altered. Our addictive demands must be exchanged for love and understanding. It is the clanging of the emotion-backed circuits in our bio-computer that keeps us disappointed, frustrated and suffering if the happenings outside do not exactly correspond to our inside programs. This condition causes conflict individually, in families and in society at large. We must constantly remind ourselves that our thoughts make us what we are. Our mental attitude is the x-factor that determines our acts and our future. We become what we think about. We must reprogram our bio-computers from destructive and hurtful thoughts and behaviors to understanding and thoughtful kindness.

Our society has become a society of abuses. Abusive individuals make up too much of our present society. If we do not begin teaching virtues and higher conscious behaviors, our society is doomed. Domestic violence can only be stopped by this knowledge and higher conscious actions.

The bounty of this world is a Divinely Created bounty. Instead of renouncing our worldly treasures, for they are here for us to enjoy, we should recognize they are an essential part of life. They are not to be worshipped, they are not to replace God; they can not get in the way of the true reality of the Almighty Universal Power. Instead, we must renounce our emotion-backed addictions and demands that keep us from enjoying the great bounties of life that have always been available around us. One who is seeking the progression into the higher conscious levels will "see" proper opportunity and be rewarded with all the richness of life.

We must be aware of the power games people play. We must beware lest confrontation arise that increases hostility. Remember to stay away from life's games that create subject-object types of separateness. Our energy will increase enormously as we give up guarding various manifestations of our security, sensation and power addictions. One of the bonuses of higher consciousness is that when we give it all up, then we get the good part back. We give up our addictive ego demands and we get back more of everything than we need to have order and happiness in our lives. As we move into the next or fifth level of consciousness, the realm of unconditional acceptance, we open doors we never could have opened when we operated from the lower four levels.

When our egos and rational minds use lower consciousness programming, they continually keep our lives from working in ways that produce optimal enjoyment. The lower levels of ego-driven manipulations constantly cause problems and negative results in our lives.

Since the ego is part of the human idea system, we must engage it to help us root out our addictions and up-level them to preferences, thus reducing ego power. We realize that our egos trigger a feeling of uneasiness when the outside world does not fit our addictive models of how it should be

We also get a flush of pleasure when the outside world does fit our addictions. In either case, our egos give us the emotional experiences that enable us to become aware of our addictive demands and to understand the heavy price we pay for them sooner or later if they are not reprogrammed into preferences. When we are in a healthy condition of personal preferences, the spiritual values kick in. They give us a new zest for life, more life, a richer more satisfying life. We will soon have greater faith, hope and courage. Eventually, the ego is put to rest.

Our ego has a part to play in revealing the addictions we have yet to work on. The ego out of control in the four lower levels develops a constant path of destruction and failure. Lower level consciousness driven by the ego is incapable of spiritual, courteous behavior. Our decaying society and its negative behaviors are caused by the lack of spiritual/virtue within. We as individuals, one-by-one empowered by virtues and values, produce goodness in ourselves and eventually society at large. Gain the connectors of Universal Energy!

WHEN WE REPROGRAM OUR ADDICTIONS TO INNER REALITY, OUR EGO WILL AUTOMATICALLY STOP TRIGGERING NEGATIVE EMOTIONS THAT INTERFERE WITH OUR HAPPINESS. THE KEY IS TO DESTROY OUR EGO-DRIVEN BEHAVIORS AND REPLACE THEM WITH SPIRITUAL KNOWLEDGE WE NEED TO GROW INTO THE HIGHER CONSCIOUSNESS. HEALTHY SPIRIT EQUALS A HEALTHY SELF-ESTEEM.

The process through the levels of conscious understanding to a greater life is possible to everyone who dedicates themselves to becoming the person they were created to be. I believe everyone in this great day of knowledge should reach with all their heart and soul for the dignity and nobleness of life. A humble healthy soul is essential.

The exciting part of the progress starts as we go into the fifth level. One should recognize by now that the four lower levels are materialistic in nature and not dependable for the true harmonies and fulfillment of life. Once again, they are necessary functions of the human endeavor but we must clear out all addictions related to them. It's time to move up!

The mighty transition about to take place in your life is the wonderful paradigm shift from materialistic lower level thought, ego-driven response and action behavior to a spiritual, harmonious lifestyle. It brings about the total fulfillment of life itself, the virtuous harmonies of wholeness and accomplishment. The quantum consciousness in life comes when we open up our own being to develop total or unconditional love. In order to develop love, universal, personal or cosmic, one must accept the whole situation of life as it is, both the good and bad. One must not only open oneself to life, we must truly communicate with it. Emerson said, "**He who is in love is wise and is**

becoming wiser, drawing from it with his eyes and mind the virtues it possesses."

The lower aspects of life are painful, shallow, disturbing and frustrating. Many are addicted to them. It is time to mature. For the sake of the real you, for all the people around you, it is time to rise to your true, free and joyful self. As we move out of ego-driven, painful addictions to the real you, remember you were created a noble person. Learn love! It is God's freeing agent! Let's go for it!

The great transition level that develops peace and harmony, love and understanding is <u>Unconditional Love</u>.

UNCONDITIONAL LOVE

Unconditional love is the fifth level of consciousness. In this level, the world begins to open up to us. The fifth level transcends subject-object relationships and we begin to see the world with the feelings and harmonies of flowing acceptance. We begin to see ourselves in everyone and everyone in ourselves. We feel compassion for the suffering of those caught in the dramas of <u>survival</u>, <u>security</u>, <u>sensation</u> and <u>power</u>. We begin to love and accept everyone unconditionally - even ourselves. It is time to let go and let God. It is time for daily meditation and prayer.

Love and relationships are universally experienced aspects of everyday life that can lead to either attachment or liberation. The highest quality of love is a liberating quality; one must be careful not to develop the addictions of attachment. Love is a force that connects to every true strand of the universe, an unconditional state that characterizes human nature; it is the true essence of the human being. Love is also a form and path of knowledge that is always there for us if only we can open ourselves to it. The paths of love are paved with virtues that skillfully cultivate patience, generosity, discipline, integrity, kindness, caring and many other virtues that will activate our daily lives. Love introduces justice and giving. They, in turn, produce the essence of life itself.

Our present society produces, by its negative attitude and nature, a force that causes depression. Depression is caused by a fear that we are lost, miscast in a world we do not understand. Depression and hopelessness are healed in a world of love accomplished by 5th level characteristics. We find we are relational beings where close loving association with others is the most effective way of trust, self confidence and security that relieves us from anxiety and depression. One of the causes of depression is separation. Agape Love is the answer!

The liberating potential of love and relationships has many facets. Love in relationships can operate as a mysterious source of growth. It offers us a glimpse of the absolute truth of life. Through love we can learn to let go of addiction and habit. Unconditional love is the gateway to discovering the importance and the gifts of the higher levels of human potential through this new consciousness. One of the most important aspects of unconditional love is that it becomes the great unifier and develops opportunities for self-knowledge and inner peace.

Love comes with the unconditional acceptance of everyone and everything around us. How do we do this? We must forgive ourselves of all past negative acts. We must forgive others their acts against us. We will then be able to grow into this powerful consciousness of unconditional love. FORGIVE ALL! When our consciousness advances and lives in the unconditional love level, we instantly accept everything else, but the acceptance is on a spiritual basis. We no longer have the need to get emotionally upset by others or ourselves. Regardless of what someone does or says we can respond with unconditional love by transcending <u>survival</u>, <u>security</u>, <u>sensation</u> and <u>material power</u> addictions. The early gift of maturing in this level is the relief of emotional dictates. We are advancing toward wellness of body, mind and spirit. Let the old stuff go!

The fifth level is the transformation level from lower consciousness to the higher levels. This level must be nearly perfected before we will reap the harvest of the higher levels. This level is also considered by many to be the most important because with its loving power one rids themselves of all prejudice, hatred and judgments against their fellow man. Only then will we, as individuals, rise up to the accomplishments of our purpose in this life. We are ready to rid ourselves of addictive negative thinking that causes negative addictive behavior.

Only our emotional programming can disturb us when the events outside do not conform to old addictions we have inside. As our old addictions melt away, we begin to experience everything and everyone around us in a different way. We no longer view people in terms of how they meet our addictive needs. We become more understanding of other's lives. When we consciously notice the hollowness and sufferings these old addictions cause, we achieve insights that further help us to get free from them. As we lose these needs, the ability and conditions of love begin to grow. We now realize that each individual has the need and the right to be doing exactly what they are doing at that time. We are learning love. Love is comforting to all parties. Love is powerful. Loving God is essential! Believe it, love is the answer! Caring and loving empowers who? YOU!

We know we have arrived in the consciousness of unconditional love when we accept the activities and actions of others as part of their journey toward spiritual awakening. We know if they are consciously on this path, they too will grow to the higher levels of human essence and peaceful co-existence. If they are not growing in their consciousness and they become angry, their violence, dislikes and hatreds no longer affect us. As our addictions become raised to preferences, we begin to find that we can instantly accept what was previously unacceptable emotionally. We do not challenge them to argue but quietly try to find solutions.

Every experience we have with other people either leaves us peaceful and loving or it makes us aware of our remaining addictions to be reprogrammed. When we win a battle of consciousness within ourselves there is nothing wrong with giving ourselves a little pat on the back because we are living more and more in the love level. The goal is to use our controlled ego to constantly raise our center of consciousness.

We must always keep in mind that if we feel love is a will to possess, it is not love. We will now become aware that no one else can rid us of the ego-driven addictive negative behaviors. No one but the real you can rise up to your potential, it will come by your own will and choice.

As we learn to live increasingly in the level of unconditional love, we begin to find we are creating a New World, a new environment in which our consciousness and our being reside. <u>People and conditions no longer are a threat to us - no one can threaten our preferences, they can only threaten our addictions</u>. Even though others may be stuck in the lower levels of consciousness, they seldom find us in that same place. We begin to help other people as they see us live in the more joyous realms of consciousness. These experiences will plant the seeds of awakening in them. The transition toward the reality of our spiritual being is now becoming obvious. The human - Godly virtues are now assisting in the development of our preferences, therefore our actions. Love absolutely dwells within all humanity. With the knowledge gained in this level we will realize the greatest freedoms that life has in store. We recognize that loving releases us from the prison of self. The freedom from self is a gift of an All-Mighty Creator. LOVE!

We begin to see with insight the worldly dramas of addictions that people are playing out on the first four levels of consciousness and we can feel compassion toward those who are still involved in the illusion of separateness. We learn the best way to help them is to work on ourselves so that they can perceive, perhaps for the first time in their lives, the experience of unconditional love. We want them to realize here is someone who accepts them all the time - no matter what they do or say. Love doesn't require that we get involved in others' problems as they struggle through life seeking survival, security, sensations and power. We just accept them because they are there, because they have a right to be there and because where they are is as perfect for their growth as where we are for ours. We may however, in a kindly loving way let them know the importance of love and growth.

This openness begins to let us flow and experience life in an almost miraculous way. When we are open, most of life's situations, which appeared to be problems, now find beautiful solutions. Love is the answer! All problems have spiritual solutions.

Love absolutely dwells within all humanity! God is love! Therefore, God dwells within. Recognize this truth.

LIFE IN REALITY IS A SERIES OF OPPORTUNITIES!

We are continually faced with a series of great opportunities, brilliantly disguised as unsolvable problems. Develop an awareness to them!

Now events are seen in terms of results and happenings instead of people's supposed attitudes toward us. We are no longer threatened by ego's false programming. The benefits to us and to the world of humanity by loving thoughts and acts are endless. People who have things to teach us, but from whom we have closed ourselves off, now can come into our lives. We willingly and happily open ourselves to more people and life situations. Loving thoughts and new understandings diminish many of our perceived conflicts in life. Instead of shying away from people and situations as we have done in the past, we now realize there is nothing to fear. Most everyone has something positive to offer if we give them a chance. It is important to regain trust, and we do.

We begin to find friendships we could not have found before. We find that people of different lands are more similar to us than different and the differences are interesting. Old prejudices break down. We start to "feel" the most powerful form of energy one can generate. <u>We are finally connecting with the Infinite source of all energy and knowledge: The Creator!</u> **Universal energy is granted to us when we discover that the whole creation and love dwells within us. O' don't worry, you will not get wings or halos.**

When we learn <u>to love ourselves and others unconditionally</u>, we no longer are addicted to slow suicide by tobacco, drugs or alcohol. We have come far from the realm of self-destruction. When we fill our soul and heart with love, bodily addictions are eliminated. The power to replace addictions, even drugs and alcohol, comes from the Holy Spirit and God's love for humankind. <u>Where a healthy spirit resides addictions cannot stay.</u>

The love of Universal Power and our fellow man will wipe away addictions. Through the higher consciousness of unconditional love and under-standing we recognize we are connected to everyone and everything around us.

To hold on to the addictions of prejudice, judgment and condemnation of any living being is nothing more than personal condemnation.

As we mature in the fifth level of unconditional love, we find we enjoy touching people more. We enjoy the beautiful feelings of warmth and oneness when we make contact not only with words, sight and sound but also through touch. As we break through the illusion of duality and separation, we begin to realize it was only our ego that previously kept us from loving people unconditionally.

It is in this level that we realize and experience "work" as an expression of love and caring. "Work" no longer is performed unconsciously or mechanically with the feeling that one cannot fully enjoy life again until the job is done. Work becomes worship to the progress of divine purpose for humankind. The rewards are great! The healing of body, mind and soul is now taking place. Work for the betterment of mankind is worship to a Universal Creator.

We increase our growth into higher consciousness by learning to meet the needs of others as though they were our own. To paraphrase an ancient saying, **"When I don't know who I am, I serve no one around me; when I do know who I am, I am one with everyone around me and their happy servant."**

Selfless service is a beautiful way to get free of the lower centers of consciousness. An oversized ego grasping for survival, security, sensation and power will always barter energy for something that will best enhance its mirage-like lower level situation. When we only do those tasks that are pleasant, unavoidable, or which we think will enhance our lower senses, we let our oversized ego keep us trapped. Selfless service without thought of reward is a characteristic of the fifth level of consciousness.

We begin to realize that living in a world of unconditional love is always enough. We know our feelings of isolation, separation and paranoia are created artificially by our emotional programming. We realize that although our bodies and minds are different, in the realm of unconditional love all of us are the same. We can return love no matter what a person does or says. When you are maturing in the fifth level, you can finally have real love and understanding for everyone because your soul has been cleansed from selfishness, prejudice and pride.

Remember; addictions waste our energy, they blind us from truth and they separate us from others. **MISUSE OF THE MIND AND SPIRIT IS NO LONGER ALLOWED!**

> IN THIS FIFTH LEVEL REALM WE EXPERIENCE PEOPLE AND SITUATIONS AROUND US AS PART OF A WORLD THAT CONSTANTLY OFFERS US EVERYTHING WE NEED. WE LIVE IN A LOVING ENERGY FIELD IN WHICH PEOPLE LOVE AND HELP US. A LOVING PERSON LIVES IN A LOVING WORLD - A HOSTILE PERSON LIVES IN A HOSTILE WORLD. EVERYONE WE MEET IS A MIRROR.

Love is a powerful and mysterious force that can take us beyond ourselves toward spiritual freedom and maturity. This liberating spirit of love reveals our deeper dimensions for self-knowledge, inner understanding and greater intimacy of life. When we affirm love and forgiveness as part of our real self, we release in our body great energy and the sacred flow within us. In the wonderful realm of forgiveness, we know we are in a process of choices. Our words, our actions and our very breath shape our rise to a better life by living in our higher consciousness. Loving is essential if we are to be fulfilled and grow to maturity. Love, giving and caring is the foundation of every healthy, harmonious relationship.

Love is also the foundation of every aspect that fundamentally and positively shapes our lives. The wellness of our very soul depends on love. Love abides in all of us, but only grows and heals where soft and tender souls reside. Let love abound in you. If hardness keeps love out, forgive others and yourself and love will shine in you. Love brings joy and allows you to grow toward a higher consciousness and capability. Start to develop a vision of selflessness and you will mature in the four higher levels. You will be truly free.

As we constantly and joyously progress in our fifth level maturity, one will not become discouraged. The energies developed by the fifth level quest are God-like and powerful. This level is not about perfection, it is concerned with maturity. Go for it! Every moment!

Let us examine these words from C. S. Lewis concerning fundamentalism and fear, which is, of course, the opposite of the wonderful confidence that is produced within our being by the higher levels:

"To love at all is to be vulnerable. Love anything, and your heart will certainly be wrung and possibly be broken. If you want to make sure of keeping it intact, you must give your heart to no one, not even to an animal. Wrap it carefully round with hobbies and luxuries; avoid all entanglements; lock it up safe in the casket or coffin of your selfishness. But in that casket - safe, dark, motionless, airless - it will change. It will not be broken; it will become unbreakable, impenetrable, and irredeemable. The alternative to love is damnation."

Think upon these thoughts:

Life is a constant interchange between human will and Divine Providence. Learn to give.

In compassion we learn to bond with the soul of others.

Unconditional Love is the great lever by which the world will be lifted to its human maturity!

We will now move into the wonderful spiritual place of the sixth level - <u>Conscious Reality</u>, a place in human growth where we really feel the maturing of the world around us. <u>Let Go</u>! <u>Rise Up</u>! Be a part of truth!

REMEMBER

1. The Creator connected everything. NO SEPARATION!

2. Think globally — **universal love** — we are all interconnected, a part of the universe in Creation.

3. Everyone is a part of the same community.

4. Do not allow your ego to separate you from goodness.

5. We are moving out of selfishness, no fear, all love!

6. Clear out the additions (anything obsessive).

7. Drop all obstacles (develop preference).

8. Rise up to your intended purpose.

9. Gain wisdom and knowledge through divine discernment and understanding. Always positive imaging!

It may surprise you that Learning through your spirit channels is much quicker and vast than the intellectual process. Go to a quiet place and think.

CONSCIOUS REALITY

Conscious Reality is the sixth level of consciousness. When our consciousness is *illuminated* by the aspects of the sixth level, we experience the friendliness of the world we are creating. We begin to realize that we have always lived in the conscious possibility of excellence - in the image of God (the image of God lies in the recognition of the foundation of spirituality: Virtues, Values Principals and Morality). To the degree we still have addictions, the perfection lies in the experience and ability we now have to get free of our emotion-backed demands. As we reprogram our addictions, we experience this perfection as a continuous enjoyment of the "precious present" in our lives.

As we become more loving and accepting, the world becomes a "horn of plenty" that gives us more than we need. We increasingly are "gifted" with a **conscious** reality that develops discernment and provides the process to recognize truth. We learn love, spiritual truth, and justice are the cornerstones of all that is good and productive. These virtues are empowered by the Spirit of an Almighty Creator.

In this level of conscious reality we find stability. Stability is, in fact, one of the important gifts of reaching the sixth level. We should now understand the power of the fifth level to transform and cleanse the spirit and the mind. At this growth level, we should clearly recognize that the greatness the fifth level provides is the dumping of all of the personal garbage and smallness in our lives. Remember: Reality does not care for the petty quarrels of men. In this sixth level, we have unconditional love strengthened with the stabilizing ability to focus on the ever-important present. We are able to keep the contamination from the past or anxieties about the future from interfering with the present. **We are truly developing total wellness.**

> AT THIS JUNCTURE ONE MUST DEPART FROM ANY RESISTANCE THAT WOULD HINDER THE WONDERFUL GROWTH THAT YOU ARE NOW EXPERIENCING. WE MUST BECOME CONSTANT AND LOVING STUDENTS OF OUR SELF AND THE WORLD AROUND US.

In the sixth level, we begin to experience our life as one positive happening after another. We now understand this transformation could have happened anytime in our lives. We begin to see this miracle of life was always there, but we could not "see" it because we were too involved with our addictions trying to manipulate people and things around us. Life offers us the full bounty of the Creators promise. Our rewards for reaching the maturity of the sixth level of consciousness are immediate. Our ego is now controlled by our spiritual self — the real you.

Little problems do not exist. We only see the solution. Humbleness creates better vision to see our true self.

During this process, we begin to experience our lives from any combination of the first six levels or all of them. In each of the six levels, we continually judge ourselves. We compare our thoughts and actions with a certain level of consciousness to determine whether we are meeting the standards of that level.

Each level presents us with a challenge: first, surviving; second, achieving security; third, experiencing sensations; fourth, developing material power; fifth, attaining the ability to love and accept everyone and everything unconditionally no matter what happens; and sixth, experiencing the friendliness and maturing of everything around us. What you "see" (your own thoughts and imaging) is what you get. By now, working day by day, your thoughts should be all positive; your results the same. **Negative emotion is ego-driven addiction. Love and understanding are the answer.**

Stability, generated by 5th and 6th level knowledge, gives us the anchor to real advancement. In this level, we come to the realization that all negative thoughts, feelings, attitudes or actions toward our immediate family members, relatives, friends, associates and people that we meet must be totally negated or discarded for the benefit of all concerned. We now realize negative thoughts disturb our own psyche or self. They contribute to our own pain and suffering and produce obstacles that get in the way of our growth and progress.

In this level we neutralize combat and anger by loving and caring. We look for win-win solutions, for everyone is a human being in need. We are all God's children — no matter how we act. We become open, relieved of the disturbing waste of prejudice, conflict and negative thinking. Even a so-called enemy is best handled with higher four level energy and behaviors. The whole world, as well as all of creation is one family, if only they knew.

Although our growth toward higher consciousness is associated by unconditionally accepting ourselves and others, we experience each of the first six levels of consciousness as a standard by which we measure ourselves. This in itself is an addiction. Each of these levels can keep us vulnerable to fear, resentment, anger, anxiety and worry. Although our consciousness has reached new highs in love and stability, we continue to worry and struggle.

To become free of these anxieties we must advance to the next level of consciousness. From this day forward, the true measure of success is how well we build our spiritual knowledge for the true benefit of self and others. We must send love into our society. We are the responsible individuals. Sixth level stability exists because your ability to unconditionally love is growing. **This sixth level of Conscious Reality is also the window of the harmony of life.**

THE LOVING, POSITIVE CARING, KIND, EMPATHETIC ATTITUDES AND IN-DEPTH CONDITIONS HAVE BEEN CAUSED BY THE SPIRITUAL GROWTH DESCRIBED IN THE FIFTH AND SIXTH LEVELS. WE MUST FOCUS AND CONCENTRATE DAILY ON THE WONDERMENT OF LIFE, THE JOY OF LIE AND THE WHOLENESS OF SELF THAT PROPELS US TO THESE EUPHORIC STATES OF THE SEVENTH AND EIGHTH LEVELS OF CONSCIOUSNESS. LIFE IS GRAND! YOU ARE LIVING IN THE CREATOR'S DESIGN. HOLD TIGHT TO YOUR NEW VISIONS OF YOUR LIFE! **THE REAL YOU!**

In this wonderful - spiritual level, when we conduct our lives with the virtues and morality prescribed by the Almighty One who created the universe, our lives become more fulfilled. We must however be cautious and work on our ego. The ego can no longer be in command. We must not act as the ego deems appropriate. If our ego demands we look outward for solutions, our heart, mind and soul must put ego to rest and look inward. For ego is nothing more than a false idea function, a liar of the first degree.

<u>We are maturing to the point where solutions are recognizable by looking into our own respected and honored beings</u>. We now "see" and experience the wonderful environments of our own life we have designed and carried forward. Our thoughts, words and actions exemplify to all how we <u>prefer</u> to live. Our harmonious preferences produce the flexibility we accept to make life more fluid or to flow in peaceful loving ways. All this is "Common Sense," our innate spiritual sense.

Remember that we must constantly review and work to perfect our unconditional love level for it is the empowerment and provides the capabilities of our growth toward our human capacity. As we ascend into the recognition of the higher levels, we must remind ourselves to stay intellectually and spiritually open. Any prejudice, addiction or emotional programming will hinder our development. We still have work to do. The next great level is <u>Conscious Awareness</u>.

REMEMBER

1. Seek God.
2. Oneness of Humanity.
3. Your real power tool is LOVE & CARING.
4. You are stabilized.
5. No more addictions
6. Emotional control by spiritual growth, TRUTH, not a religious box.
7. Recognize obstacles to maturity. Run them over like they are not there.
8. Stay flexible and open.
9. Love yourself and others. NO MATTER WHAT!

Commit
Yourself
To
The
Courage
To
Advance
Into
This
New
And
Wonderful
Place!

CONSCIOUS AWARENESS

Conscious Awareness is the seventh level of consciousness. In this level, we are finally liberated from the bondage of anxiety and fear. Our conscious awareness allows us to watch our body and mind perform in the lower levels. This is a meta-level from which we non-judgmentally witness the drama of our body and mind and their activities. We don't pat ourselves on the back or criticize ourselves in any way. We just blissfully enjoy the show of life.

From this glorious non-prejudicial center, we learn to impartially observe our social roles and life gains from a place within us that is free from fear, anxiety and vulnerability. In this level, we do not judge or evaluate; we just witness ourselves. We use the conscious awareness level as a meta-center from which we experience every moment of our lives from that deep, calm place inside where we observe everything and accept it. This seventh level is a blissful state of personal satisfaction and the recognition of the God within which provides us with total and peaceful confidence. We start to realize we are a wonderful creation of God. <u>We stop our false imaging of ourselves</u>.

This level provides space between us and the surrounding world. From this <u>detached conscious awareness</u> level we just watch ourselves performing in all the levels of life. We no longer are vulnerable to ups and downs. Nothing can disturb us or bring us down, even though our body and minds may be going through various types of drama. Our emotions and consciousness can stay in this protected and beautiful place deep inside us where everything is peaceful, even if our body or minds go through a manifestation of anger or jealousy. We now realize we are only playing out one of our addictive roles. NO ADDICTIONS!

The human being, the Creator's most marvelous creation, is finally becoming free. The spiritual recognition of our own capacities and capabilities through the activities of the higher levels has now given us the recognition of our spiritual greatness. In the wonderful world of conscious awareness, we can now go to the peaceful quiet place within ourselves each day. We empty our minds of all thought and experience stillness. We must stay acquainted with our true self. For in the deep still place within we find energy, knowledge flow, joy, harmony and peace.

When we go to that peaceful place within, we realize our true relationship, our oneness with the universe and all its powers. We will discover that in that deep center of our being dwells the spirit of universal reality. We then know that all possibility dwells within our very self. We "see" the unified field and the energy of love empowering our lives and activities. We "feel" and become sensitive to our real self and the universe. All things are possible. This knowledge leaves out nothing. Take a deep breath; be at peace for Universal Energy is increasing in your whole being.

You are now realizing the essence of the real you. Your ego-driven false deceptive programming is gone — you are becoming you. Stress and distress are no longer factors, for when they come we know where and how to go to that quiet place within. You no longer allow other people or things to have power over you. No one can ruin your day. Let the idea of limitations and boundaries go. **You will find comfort and peace. Life is grand! Your soul is healing! Your soul is maturing.**

We still have to "chop wood and carry water" and be productive in our life regardless of the level of consciousness we have achieved. Now, more than ever, we want to play an active part in the world around us. We start to develop visions of the truth of ourselves and eventually the whole planet. We will develop "universal sight." We open up to learning, interacting with people and doing our part in building more beautiful surroundings, and in assisting the advancement of a New World by living a conscious life. You are now among the living-living, instead of the living-dead, which constitutes a majority of the world's population. You are much more than biologically alive.

However, the world's condition is changing rapidly as these new conscious levels that raise human esteem are being recognized. **We all can achieve solid inner peace.** We must view everything we do and say as part of our growth toward conscious awareness and inner peace. We must constantly strive to say and do positive things, to think positive thoughts. This will reinforce our progress. When humankind learns these truths, peace on earth will become a reality through the collective efforts of all knowing people.

A higher conscious person cannot, by their very nature, cause war or kill, steal, rape or hurt another. They know that what they do to other people they are really doing to themselves. These people know who they are. We should all strive to fulfill our lives. Fulfillment cannot be achieved until we reach higher conscious awareness.

Our addictive programs that activate our ego and rational mind constantly keep us from realizing who we really are. The way to tell "who we think we are" is to notice carefully what our ego is guarding. What are the "fronts" or social images that we are in the progress of living out. What triggers anger, fear, jealously or grief? Which "somebody" does our rational mind defend? **One should not take up the habits that cause us to defend ourselves.** Whatever acts we are portraying and reinforcing with our ego represent whom we think we are. **We must know who we really are.** Spiritual, higher level imaging reveals the real created you. With this recognition of the real you, harmony and personal progress is a natural.

False programming no longer keeps us vulnerable and insecure. When we recognize our addictions that cause us to be an angry, fearful or jealous person, we begin to engage them and denounce them with a loving, understanding and compassionate consciousness represented in the fifth through eighth levels. We then establish an inner peace through unconditional love and conscious awareness.

Our real self begins to appear. We finally begin to know ourselves in truth. The actual image of Divine Creation begins to shine in our countenance. We become real persons with virtuous driving mechanisms. We recognize our divine virtuous self; loving, giving and humble. The seventh level of **conscious awareness** provides the peace and tranquility needed for the further advancement of humankind.

We still travel on occasion into the realms of **survival, security, sensation and power**. However, obsessive or unhealthy ventures in these realms no longer occur because the lower four levels are now in our control. We have conscious control because we now live in the upper realms of human consciousness and potential.

These upper realms include the fifth level of **unconditional love** where we accept everyone and everything around us; the sixth level of conscious reality where we experience the friendliness of the world we are creating; and the seventh level of conscious awareness where we finally are free of life's struggles. We can partake without the emotional trauma and we can impartially observe our social roles from a place that is free from fear and vulnerability.

When we live in the seventh level of consciousness, we are ready to transcend self-awareness and become **pure awareness**. We truly find the perfection in human creation. Think spiritually. The essential you is perfect, has always been perfect, and always will be perfect! There is nothing you can do to alter the perfection of the essential you. Once it is uncovered you will know this is the image of special creation, NOT OUR IMAGINED SELF!

The essence of humankind, our spiritual conscious being is the soul of mankind. You are no longer addicted. Love, wisdom and oneness characterize your actions. You recognize the spiritual connected aspects of all people. You are a joyful being. You have the power of divine discernment. You no longer accept ignorance, dogma, ritual or superstition. **You are an exemplar of spiritual virtues.**

> THE SPIRITUAL GROWTH REPRESENTED BY THIS LEVEL PRODUCES A KIND, GENTLE, CARING, SYMPATHETIC, UNDERSTANDING AND LOVING PERSON. THE REWARDS ARE ENDLESS - WISDOM, KNOWLEDGE, TRUE UNDERSTANDING AND DIVINE DISCERNMENT ARE AMONG THE MOST TRULY POWERFUL GIFTS. THE HARMONY OF LIFE IS ANOTHER. WE ARE MATURING!

You are intellectually, spiritually and physically healthy; the essence of wholeness and wellness. You are detached from the mundane behaviors of a world caught up in the four lower levels. You must remain, under all conditions, humble and kind for your real security and peace lie within these factors. You are a contributor to the advancement of the human condition when your personal Universal connectors are constant. **Pure awareness** develops without dogma, ritual and superstition. Virtues and Truth replace them.

Your subconscious mind and spirit have been perfecting in the **pure conscious** level that is governed by universal law. All the peoples of the world to one degree or another, are wanting to mature in these four supreme and high levels of natural human consciousness. The highest recognizable level of human conscious capability is described as the <u>Ultimate Universal Conscious Level or Pure Consciousness</u>.

<u>ULTIMATE UNIVERSAL CONSCIOUS LEVEL</u>

Ultimate Universal Conscious Level is the eighth level of consciousness. At this ultimate level, we are one with everything. We are love, peace, energy, beauty, wisdom, clarity, truth, justice and oneness. We are one with our Creator, His prophets, humankind and the world around us! We realize by tuning into the ocean of loving energy that is around us, we have more security, enjoyable sensations, effectiveness and love than we ever need for a continuously beautiful life. We now enjoy the dramas of our lives and the excellent spiritual beings that we naturally are. **We have become givers of the universe.**

In this eighth level of consciousness, we are catapulted from self-awareness to the perfection of **pure awareness**. We no longer witness or judge ourselves. The body, mind, senses and **conscious awareness** are not separated. We are finally whole. In this ultimate level, we do not experience survival, security, sensations, power, love and conscious reality, we embrace and enjoy survival, security, sensations, power, and love as the fullness of life. We have absolute healthy self-esteem. **We can discern the truth of all things. Discernment is the power to know truth.**

You now know the true meaning of God's holy words. No human being is allowed to keep us in any box causing ignorance or control. **We are in harmony with the Universe.** We are the knowers of truth - the truth that had been promised which would set us free. We are blessed with vision, wisdom and knowledge. Reprogramming the "self" attains the highest state of consciousness. Our thought activity is calmed to spiritual truth. Our recognition of justice is clear and detailed. The direction of perception has shifted from subject-object manipulation, through phases of loving acceptance, to a unity with the environments of the universe. We respect and care for Mother Nature. We excel in virtuous behavior.

At the eighth consciousness level, we function with enormous effectiveness because the screens and veils that limit our receptiveness have been eliminated. We tune into the finer nuances of our surrounding world. We are open to the broad spectrum of all the finer cues of the world we were unable to notice before because our consciousness was occupied by lower level survival, security, sensation and power addictions. Pure awareness constitutes harmonious and loving relationships. They are natural; no more conflicts that cause disharmony. <u>We are harmony</u>.

As we continue our journey to higher consciousness, we have become the essence of our real self. This does not mean that our worldly activities have become perfected, just our spiritual knowledge and behaviors. The proofs are many. At this level, we have truly achieved our birthright. As a fully conscious being, we are optimally perceptive, wise and effective. We have transcended all personal boundaries and experience, no separation from anyone or anything in the world by the act of prejudice.

Serving "others" becomes a main priority in our lives because everything is experienced from an "us" perspective. Our ability to love our enemies is a wonderful part of eighth level maturity. Now we love no matter what! Thus, we help empower toward a positive, loving world. We are gifted with detachment. We can live in an imperfect world, but it does not emotionally affect us.

The eighth or **ultimate universal level** of consciousness is not easy to attain. Be not discouraged, millions of people, though aware, have not attained its full embrace. Achieving it requires a detached lifestyle and a period of intense consciousness growth. Many addictions must be eliminated to reach this level. Although many people reach the fifth, sixth and seventh levels and enjoy life they are not one hundred percent free of the addictions. Yet, people who operate primarily from the higher levels of consciousness can, within minutes, work through whatever survival, security, sensation or power addictions are being triggered and then return to the higher levels of consciousness.

Seek the Creator, truth, justice and love with all your might and you will be granted ultimate universal knowledge and wisdom. You will be totally fulfilled. The upper levels enable us to live a happy, fulfilled, wise, effective and enjoyable life. It is important to understand the ultimate universal conscious level, yet achieving it cannot become another addiction. If we strive to use the fifth, sixth or seventh centers of consciousness in processing and interpreting our energies and those of the world around us, we will experience a deep peace and enjoyment within our hearts and souls. In this way we recognize the oneness of all humanity.

When our consciousness is living in the upper four levels, we are growing toward God, for He is manifest in us and we are one with Him. The truth of His message and His messengers become apparent. Remember that Christ said, "Seek the truth and the truth will set you free". This is the day of truth for those who can see and hear, those who are not veiled or clouded.

To a great degree, the religions of the world have been void of these truths because they are manipulated by human kind's ego-driven ideas. These truths were veiled by the ignorance and darkness of mans past. **As goes the consciousness of humankind, so goes its religion, family, nation and peace within.** The misunderstanding of these truths causes the constant divisions and separations of man's institutions, regardless of religious or social affiliation.

As we advance into the realms of truth, true reality, justice and love, we no longer are separate; we truly know we are one. As we progress, we "see" the plan of the Creator for humankind.

The image of Universal Reality is mirrored in the upper four levels of human consciousness. As our consciousness begins to dwell increasingly in the levels of **unconditional love** and **conscious reality**, we begin to develop a multi-level perception that enables us to see all our thoughts and actions from each of the levels. As we refine this multi-level awareness, we learn to witness ourselves from the seventh level, a **detached conscious awareness**. There no longer is a feeling of lower or higher consciousness, it is all the same from the **conscious awareness level**.

From this wonderful vantage place, we can be involved in all aspects of life while no emotional damage can be done. We are spiritually protected — life is a joyous positive harmony. **Truth is our real power and knowledge is our comfort.** Then we go beyond the conscious awareness level to the selfless, unified space of the ultimate universal conscious realm. Here we find the absolute truth of our being, the reason for our existence: **TO ADORE, WORSHIP AND LOVE OUR CREATOR, the Creation and our interconnected fellow human beings.**

Many believe the reach toward Universal Empowerment and higher consciousness may be restricting to their "fun" and enjoyment. Of course, the opposite is true. The only way we can attain enduring peace, prosperity, fulfillment, productive-ness, love, unity, health and happiness is from this process of truth and spiritual knowledge. The virtues constitute our real self and are a part of our creation. Virtues give us understanding of our real beings. The whole of humankind will soon be aware of this great knowledge and will begin their long overdue maturity.

Start today. Be honest with yourself, list your bad habits and addictions that have you imprisoned and in bondage. **List the behaviors that cause problems in your life. Next list the positive aspects of your higher consciousness**

of love and caring. Unconditional love is the answer to most of man's addictions. This includes the love and respect of oneself. You have a responsibility to yourself. Work on the positive side of your list until it is perfected. Improvement is always good.

Remember, addictions waste your energy; once diminished you will have a high supply of energy. Addictions blind you; once removed you will have a clearer insight into what you should do or not do in various life situations. Addictions separate you from others; they keep you from the bounties of life. When you get rid of these you will live in a loving energy field in which people love you and want to help you. You will be pleased with the real you - the person with painful addictions will be gone from your very being. Your happiness and peaceful co-existence will increase.

When these two lists are complete, destroy the half with the addictions listed. **For thirty days recopy by hand the positive list of love, respect, compassion, understanding, kindness in action, kindness of the tongue, praise to God, thankfulness for all blessings, self-respect, prosperity by works and togetherness bound by unconditional love.** To inaugurate your process of growing, maturing and becoming a whole person find immediately what charitable organization or people you can be of service too.

If you continue by this method to look in and see the wonderful realities of your own being and development of the spiritual attributes, you will be guaranteed a harmonious lifestyle. Virtues are the keys to the transformation to the real you. Do not procrastinate another moment. Today is your new beginning toward the realization of the divine, valuable, important you. **Let no one deter you from your peace and greatness, your course to fulfillment.**

REMEMBER

1. Love — No person has the right to abuse another by any means, physical, spiritual, emotional or economic.
2. Oneness of humanity — We are all leaves on different branches of one tree.
3. Wellness — Body, mind (intellect), spirit and soul — all must be well.
4. Rights — Recognize the rights of all men, women and children
5. Knowledge through education — Knowledge causes individuals to excel.
6. Remove your labels — Accept Yourself. No more negative names that program addictions.
7. You are already whole! — Believe it, you were created as an extension of a the greatest creation. You do not have to prove yourself to anyone. Excellence comes from within assisted by knowledge.
8. Seek spiritual riches — Virtues, values, principles and morality — God's riches enrich your life.
9. Spend quiet time meditating and praying – Spiritual learning starts with conversing with the Creator of this marvelous universe.

Free at last, Free at last, thank you GOD I am Free at last!

> **MAY YOU USE YOUR UNDERSTANDING OF YOUR TRUE HUMAN ESSENCE TO PROMOTE THE UNITY AND TRANQUILITY OF HUMANKIND, TO GIVE ENLIGHTENMENT TO THE PEOPLE YOU MEET, TO PRODUCE LOVE ALL AROUND YOU AND TO ASSIST IN BRINGING ABOUT UNIVERSAL PEACE. IN THIS MANNER I AM SURE THE ALMIGHTY ONE WHO CREATED THE UNIVERSE WILL SHINE UPON YOU.**

May you always have the knowledge that the essential building blocks needed in the maturing of your whole being and consciousness is to be found in the innate values and virtues. *The true power of justice and love, kindness, consideration, determination, caring understanding, trustworthiness, honesty, truthfulness and courage are but a few of the known virtues. (*Virtues section of this book.)

No matter how old you are, no matter what your past or present is, no matter your economic, religious, social, racial or health conditions: **YOU CAN BECOME THESE HIGHER LEVEL REALITIES. YOU WILL UNCONDITIONALLY LOVE THE REAL YOU!**

We must recognize it is time for humankind as a species to grow into maturity, out of our barbaric adolescence. We must recognize the importance of self-love for if we denythe love of self, we have denied God.

Self-Abuse in any way is Spiritual denial.

One must learn and teach spiritual principles so we may transcend our own needs to understand the needs of others. The soul has been given the right to soar like eagles by the word of the Almighty One. Do not act as a crippled sparrow.

Your capacity to love deepens when we tap into the silence of our innter self. Quiet meditation is one of the greatest adventures.

Enjoy the miracle of just being alive. You make your day, believe it.

This is YOU!

Regardless of the difficulties I face, I will pursue my goals joyfully with relentless determination.

No obstacle will deter my progress, no discouragements will lower my God-given enthusiasm, and no adversity will slow my progress.

I will maintain my confidence and stay adamant concerning my plans, behaviors, and life expectations.

The wonderful universe will provide my inexhaustible, spiritual energy and powers.

I will pray for spiritual illumination that centers on love and understanding.

God grant me wisdom, knowledge understanding, and discernment to live by the four pillars: virtues, values, principals and morality. Nothing is stronger for the betterment of life! Love is the driver!

No financial condition can keep me from acquiring the highest levels of

MATURE CONSCIOUSNESS! IT IS NOT ABOUT MONEY!

YOU WILL NOT BE REMEMBERED FOR THINGS YOU HAVE DONE FOR YOURSELF; YOU WILL BE REMEMBERED FOR THINGS YOU HAVE DONE FOR OTHERS.

EVERY PERSON YOU MEET IS JUST ANOTHER PRECIOUS HUMAN BEING WITH THE SAME NEEDS AS YOURSELF. THEY MAY BE AT JUST ANOTHER STATION WITH A DIFFERENT BACKGROUND OF WHICH THEY PROBABLY HAD LITTLE CHOICE. LOVE THEM AS YOU WOULD YOURSELF.

THE DECKER EIGHT CONSCIOUS LEVELS IN REVIEW

SURVIVAL

Survival is about struggle: Fear, Contest. Conflict causes fear addiction. Survival is disheartening and non-spiritual. It is the cause of blinding addictions. It starts to present an illusion of separateness and harshness, high-energy use, stresses, and distress. It causes self to be imprisoned by self. Selfishness disturbs physical and mental health. It keeps one low and ignorant. When you are survival-driven your ego is in command. Anxiety of survival produces disharmony & low self-esteem, disturbing positive attitudes. Survival is an ego-power level: NOT GOOD!

SECURITY

Material security seeking is the beginning of idol worship. Material security for self and family is healthy. Do not idolize these possessions. This level should be named false security. No real security exists in the four lower levels. All things can be gone in an instant. If we focus on this level of false security we can become addicted and our real growth is hindered.

SENSATION

Looking outside of self is dangerous to advancement. Sensation can destroy the human soul and our well being. It also has a fine side if pursued under loving ways. The false world of pain and suffering reside in low level sensation addictions. The effects of drugs etc. causes first the near death of the soul and then the body. Being addicted to anything disrupts the advancement of your true being. Use the gifts of true sensation, hearing, feeling, smelling, seeing, etc. for the betterment of life and the wonderment thereof. True sensation comes from love.

MATERIAL POWER

Greed and Ego-centric behavior and false imaging are the center points of the material power level. This level never produces enough for the power-ego driven person. It is sad that some persons addicted to this level feel they are their possessions. If these possessions go so goes the person. We are not our material possessions! People who feel they can destroy others in their greed for materialistic advancement are deeply addicted to lower level behavior. Manipulation and power control addictions finally destroys self and those around them. Obnoxious arrogance, abilities to become insensitive to others and strong addictions marks this Material Power addicted low self-esteem person.

UNCONDITIONAL LOVE

This is the main level for the maturing real person. This level is the transformation level from the lower four levels to the upper or higher levels. Here we go through a cleansing transformation of mind and spirit. Now we can dump junk. Loving energy comes in abundance where we can accept our true self and others. Learn that love is the only real emotion. All others are the result of the absence of love. The Creator is love and the source of love. Love drives out fear and ignorance. Love is the reflection of the Creator's love for us. Unconditional love allows our whole being to now assimilate the wonderful aspects of nature and the world in which we live. The fifth level must be completed before the soul & spirit can grow properly. Love thy neighbor as thyself!

CONSCIOUS REALITY

We now feel Friendly, World Stability, Precious Present Reality, Excellence, Loving Student of Self and World, and Positive Life. In this level of conscious reality we start to experience real growth. Detach from negative aspects of life. Begin to see goodness in all of creation. <u>Stop the ego demands of separation</u>

from each other and GOD. We see Reality more clearly now. It takes a very spiritual sense to see and feel it. It is not an intellectual process. Get quiet, meditate and "see" from the vision of the spirit and soul.

CONSCIOUS AWARENESS

Liberated from fear and anxiety; Out of all bondage; No longer vulnerable; Peaceful confidence; Start to recognize real self; Finds the quiet place within; We "see" our real divine self; Inner peace and tranquility. The real "Horn of Plenty" develops. Spiritual Truth can now be "seen". Spiritual Realities of life become clear. The spiritual "eye" and "ear" are opened. Wellness increases. Spiritual, Physical and Intellectual balance takes place. We start to see God in everyone and everything.

ULTIMATE UNIVERSAL CONSCIOUSNESS

Pure awareness; Free from the addictive self; Wholeness; Wellness; Constant inner joy and peace; Wisdom; Knowledge, Understanding and Divine Discernment; Harmony with God; **Spiritual truth;** Knowing Self. Develop swiftly toward wholeness and completeness. We feel the inter-connected aspects of all things. We are oneness with nature and our fellow human beings. At last perfect peace has come and we love ourselves in a healthy way! **LIFE IS FULFILLED!**

> THE CREATOR HAS DESIGNED A PURPOSE FOR ALL PEOPLE. WE HAVE THE RESPONSIBILITY TO FIND IT. ALL LIMITATIONS ARE SELF-IMAGINED; YOU ARE AN UNLIMITED BEING. YOU CAN DO WHATEVER YOU BELIEVE YOU CAN. YOUR GREATEST PURPOSE WILL ALWAYS BENEFIT OTHERS. YOU ARE A PERSON OF GREAT PURPOSE!

The more you spend time in quiet places looking into yourself; the more you will love and appreciate God's creative works, <u>KNOWING THE REAL YOU!</u>

Study Addendum

For those who wish to deepen their knowledge of the cause and effect of these very important aspects of life, we write this addendum.

To see life as a beautiful poem and yourself participating in its poetry can lead to a balance of charm and fulfillment. To develop actions that come from the vocabulary of life's great Poetry causes one to be in accord with universal harmony. To strive each day to become one with the systems of Divine Creation is the essence of life. It is actually <u>to live</u>.

To be among the living-dead is a common place to be. One must truly look into themselves, in a totally honest manner, to know where we are. We will show how one finds the good road of life and the cause and effect of certain behaviors.

Decker's Hierarchy of Human Consciousness :

As we ascend the levels of consciousness our lives mature and we become fulfilled. Our purpose is recognized. We are granted the four most important gifts: **Wisdom, Knowledge, Understanding and Divine Discernment. We have a new birth. We are finally fully alive.**

When you are at the bottom of this hierarchy, described by the lower levels of

Knowing the Real You, one cannot "see out." You are really isolated from Reality. When one gets toward the top we can "see quite well." At the top we can "see" in all directions. Our awareness becomes acute, our innate abilities come to light. From the top of the pure awareness conscious plane we see all people in a different light.

Yes, it is true we are all God's children. Many of the differences are beautiful. Many are in pain for they have been treated badly by others. Be one of the kind ones. When we reach this top, and anyone can, there the "eye of God" opens for us so we can finally "see and hear" clearly. What a great place to be! This top is not arrogant, however the oxygen is terrific. The mind and soul is so at peace. The spirit wise!

With all people, in all cultures and religions there is a basic theme, a basic purpose, universal consciousness that prevails in a timeless universal persistence. This mighty driver is awakened in the higher conscious levels. Its strong natural persistence is what really pushes us to achieve the good life of peace and harmony. It drives us to grow, mature and gain wisdom and knowledge. In this most radiant century we have advanced in a global knowledge base greater than all centuries past. You can be a part of that.

We do indeed have diverse global cultures and beliefs. People in the past have dwelled on their differences and have gone to killing wars because one side had a different belief or religion. In the maturing of the future, humankind will unite by the respect of these differences and the wonderment of our similarities. By the nature of the knowledge gained by the study of books, etc., we grow to assist in the maturing of those cultures by our own behavior.

In the maturing culture of the next generations we learn to admire both our differences and our similarities. Differences are not defects, they are wonderfully exciting places in the fabric of life. It is time to gather the great experiences of life. You can be a part of that. By this knowledge you have gained you will rise to your true and ultimate place. You are designed to do it. You will! It is a natural in this advancing age.

In the eight levels of consciousness we can attribute certain behavior with the conscious level a person is operating under. It is vital one try diligently to ascend out of the lower levels before they are caught in an addictive state. In the maturing of life each one of us goes through all of the levels. Some never get past the lower four. The maturing of a person can be painful or it can be sheer delight, the choice is really yours.

THE MATURING OF A HUMAN LIFE

In Survival we find: killing, pain, fear, low self-esteem, frustration, hatred and barbaric acts of all kinds. Low energy and bad attitudes prevail. Ignorance abounds. Harshness and abuses of all kinds exist. Sadness and lonely existence take us over. Fight and flight prevail. It is a dark place of slow advancement. Get out of it!

In Security we find: illusion, wars, killing, false beliefs, idol worship and disharmony for the sake of so called, "Security." Security without higher conscious level spirit and knowledge is no security at all. Your possessions will not establish real security. Your inner self dictates your real security. Power is also not true security.

In Sensation we find: sensation in some forms is quite acceptable. However seeking sensation for its own sake is dangerous to your good health and wellness. Many times sensation is sought by drugs, alcohol and illegal activities. The search for sensation can take us out of the realm of good virtuous conduct. It can take us away from our good responsibilities to family and friends. Be very cautious when you seek sensation. Many who are addicted to this realm start to demand separation from their own spirituality. One must always ask the question, is it good for me and those I am responsible for? Is it right for my spirit and soul? Honest questions; honest answers can save your life. Follow your true self. Do not deny it. Do not become separated from your true self.

In Material Power we find: Material Power is the most dangerous of all conscious levels. It is not to say that to have fine possessions is not acceptable. However, when these possessions become more important than our spiritual/soulful consciousness we have stopped our growth into the Real Realms of self and our eternal life may suffer along with our present conditions.

In this level we have gathered all the aspects of the four lower levels into this one most illusive fourth level. We are now able to function with harshness that is the accumulation of surviving, trying to develop security, seeking sensations and going after the greed of material power.

Arrogance is a real problem in this level. The demand of exclusiveness kills the real humbleness that is necessary for true advancement. We begin to enter into power struggles that dilute our spiritual integrity. We develop false and narrow beliefs. Our world seems to get larger because we own more when in fact our real world is shrinking. Happiness eludes us. We worship these things we own. Our family and friends can be put in the background. We buy our children and wife with more things. Gifts take the place of our spending real time and showing affection and love. More false beliefs become the daily modus operandi. Soon we worship our house and car, our boat and bank account. Our world is getting smaller.

In this conscious level prison, disease is prevalent. Emotional disorders become common place. Life becomes a truly unhappy struggle. The real problem is people think this is **normal**. This harsh world of prejudice and struggle brings about the negative influences that keep the human species from their God-given ability to advance out of their barbaric state. Without advancing into the higher levels of human possibility, the world is in fact a harsh environment. The tough guys inhabit it instead of the caring ones. It is controlled by greed, not by honest opportunity for all.

It is time to join the real people. They are happy with themselves in a very healthy way. One who is striving to learn and act in the higher consciousness does not destroy themselves in any way. No self pity, no foreign substances into the body. It will destroy the spirit first and then the body itself.

You are the essence of life. You will know it as you pass into the knowledge and wonderful world of the four higher conscious levels.

- This is the major transition in all the realms of consciousness of human advancement.

- This is the most important single step you will ever make.

- This step has never been fully taught. It is however essential to real living.

- No real fulfillment can come into a life with out this reality.

- The transition from lower level attitudes to the higher four levels takes dedication.

- Your life will change when you spend the time and effort to spiritually perfect it.

- This level had been described in all the Holy books, by all of the divine ones.

The fifth level, the fifth dimension of human consciousness is the first level of spiritual grace. It is also where we find the growing aspects of higher self-esteem. The confidence one develops in this level is of great value to a productive life. We look at Loving Unconditionally as something we give. This is true, however the receiving aspects of this level far exceed that which we give. To grow to the state where we do not judge and we give love easily to all, if only for a moment, is to have reached a noble place. You will be the one to benefit greatly by your ability to love unconditionally.

SOME BENEFITS OF AGAPE-UNCONDITIONAL LOVE

- You become a seeker of the truth.
- It sets you free!
- Your light will come on.
- You will recognize the similarities in all peoples. Difference is not a defect!
- Virtuous-like behavior is exciting.
- The transition itself is gratifying.
- IQ increases.
- Your world enlarges in a knowledge sense.
- It is the beginning of one's great enlightenment.
- You have a lot of love to give; give it.

The rewards are greater still!

In Conscious Reality we find: the true recognition and understanding of reality. Reality has two major forms. There is that reality I spell with small case. That is the one that is your own or your perceived reality. It is your concept of reality. This you have a right to. However, I would be very cautious in insisting it is actually Reality. There is an absolute Reality in the universe. It is the science of all things created. It is a spiritual realm of wisdom, knowledge, understanding and divine discernment. It takes a spiritual knowledge, a spiritual "Seeing Eye" to know this great ocean of knowledge.

You have heard some will "see and hear", the others will not know. In Conscious Reality we begin in earnest to cleanse the spirit and the bio-computer. We begin to "see" the goodness most would like to have. Our journey into a life of loving- kindness has begun.

In this wonderful place we grow to appreciate the goodness of life. We stop our separation demands against God and self. We detach ourselves from the negative aspects of life's toil. One of life's most important growth steps occurs here. Self-esteem takes a quantum leap as we are empowered by Positive Stability. It's a natural at this stage of development. You'll love it.

QUIET SPIRITUAL POWER

QUIET HUMBLE JOYOUS LOVING POWER

In Conscious Awareness we find: GREATNESS! This is a most amazing conscious level. It is the place where more and more people are trying to reach. I hope this will give you a better understanding of these practical higher levels of life and how we achieve having them become a natural part of your daily activities. We were all designed by a Creator to arrive in the depths of these wonderful Spirit Powered Realms.

Most people who are living in harmony and peaceful co-existence have reached this beautiful conscious awareness level. When you fully "see" the greatness in nature or "feel" the wonderment of a gentle breeze or appreciate the flowers and the trees you have deepened in this level.

A most amazing transformation takes place when one can mature in this place of conscious awareness. We actually become aware of the greatness of the universe around us. The wonderful nuances of the world come to life for us. It is a new-world we now see. We "see" more clearly who we really are. We no longer see ourselves as a person of low capability. Our self-esteem is getting very healthy.

In our state of peaceful confidence we are liberated from any fear and anxiety patterns we once had. It is a natural condition in this level that we are centered and balanced. We now have both feet on the ground, as they say.

Strive to spend much time in conscious awareness. It will soon become a part of your natural caring self.

<u>**In Pure Conscious Maturity we find**</u>**:** the highest possible conscious level granted to the human species. In this most great level we "see" that the image of God in mankind is a universal spiritual vastness of which we can comprehend only a small bit. As we evolve as a species more of this vast ocean will be revealed to us. We can only absorb it one drop at a time. It is of vast importance that we strive to reach this marvelous place for much is at stake.

Know for a fact people run the whole conscious plane from Survival to Pure Conscious Maturity. Your goal should be to make the lower levels a balanced given while enjoying the greatness and tranquility of the wonderful upper levels of consciousness and the activity that accompanies them. This is living, this is life itself!

Your intellect and your spirit are now working together in the development of the Real You!

This is a place you can achieve. Yes, the saints did it. Of course many other people have accomplished this most important feat. It is the essence of life and very important to your life on this earth. Your eternal being will be propelled to the maturing of your very soul.

One "sees" quite differently now. The great surprise is that you are truly given the essence of Wisdom, Knowledge, Understanding and Divine Discernment. It has been coming to you as you have grown in knowledge in knowing the real you through all the conscious levels.

In the upper four levels we "see" the whole universe and every person with a different "consciousness." For the first time, if you have reached these levels, you can experience **Universal Oneness.** We are all created from the same mold with many wonderful differences. The recognition of Universal Oneness is a sign we are growing into our real pre-ordained basic precious self.

One of the most important aspects we discover is that we are really free from the prison of self. We no longer condemn in any way. We just go on in the delightful world of peace and harmony. We take setbacks as learning environs and go right on in a cheerful manner. Life is nearly euphoric. Life is great and oh so exciting. We get to explore how life should be. What a relief!

Each person has the responsibility to strive for this gracious way of life. When you do you become a part of the growing maturity of the mass of civilization. As each person adds to the critical mass to develop true knowledge and goodness we decrease the negative elements of society. These people who have grown to enjoy living in the REAL WORLD of upper conscious levels become the positive empowering society of global harmonious growth. Yes, it is underway if you can "see" now.

How would you like to live in a world where these things prevail on consistent bases? This should become a part of your new daily planning.

The important aspect of what you take in is the ability to apply divine discernment to filter and reject the junk. I don't think you would have much left to put in your permanent storage. One thing we must learn is to keep the junk out. Why take it in? It has no real value to the advancement of your life or the goodness therein.

Now your destiny is in your hands!

Now you are at peace with yourself!

Your world evolves around a set of universal thoughts, actions and deeds. They benefit not only yourself but everyone around you. You grow into a condition were you not only seek the good things, you are the spiritually good things. Life is wonderful and fulfilling.

In the upper levels of living you are:

- **Justice**
- **Love**
- **Virtues**
- **Values**
- **Principals**
- **Fairness**
- **Harmony**
- **Joy & Peace**

When you reside in the upper realms of your true self you no longer reach for these attributes: You are these and more. Life has reached a blissful state you never knew existed. You did not know it was attainable, but in truth it was always a part of your real innate self. You are no longer the judge and jury of the world. You are an understanding being recognizing that we all have serious work to do in the wonderful realms of growing into mature human beings. No one is perfect we all have problems of different sorts. We are truly meant to be our brother's keeper. To assist as often as we can to help our fellow human beings. Selfishness will only bring pain and suffering.

It is time to reach out and help someone. Find a worthwhile project and volunteer. The results will aid you in your spirit quest for your joyful ascension in finding the real you! Be a joyful positive being! It will bring you life!

These eight distinct levels of conscious behavior are a part of you just as much as your arm or leg. They are as sure as your heart and lungs. They have fundamental function in your everyday life.

In Decker's Hierarchy of Human Conscious Levels we find the cause and effect of operating in certain areas of human consciousness. It is important to know that all levels are connected and one can use several at one time. One can jump from one to another quite quickly. In the maturing of humankind we find more and more people are striving to understand and rise to the fine air of the higher levels. This will become common place in this millennium.

As knowledge increases we evolve upward into this spirit of maturity. Harshness and complacency are replaced by the caring attributes of Virtues, Values, Principals and Morality. It is important that we get into a spiritual journey and not be misled by religious exclusivity or false doctrine.

Be also assured your fun will not be hindered by your growing into the fullness of your self. You already are all of the levels. It is part of your innate being. All that is happening here is you are finding your great capacity and bringing it into the fruits by the seeds you already have. Finding the real you can be at first difficult. You may have so much false illusion to deal with it may take some time to peel it off. It may cause some pain to recognize that other people have put false beliefs upon you. Many people can inflict serious wounds into another with illusion and lies. You will discover in every person lies the highest conscious level.

You are a child of Universal Creation. This we can say without exception. In that reality you will find you are a capable divine being ready to prepare for the next stage of your eternal trip. Enjoy the greatness of life offered here on this planet. Demand of yourself the fullness of this life. Rise up to your purpose and potential. Live in the higher levels provided for you by the Greatest Spirit. If this were not true you would not exist. Nor would the ground you walk on. **You are a very important part of this vast universe if only you knew. Knowledge is the key to Knowing, be a SEEKER!**

When we experience insight, self-acceptance and learn to love ourselves, new possibilities are truly endless.

When we experience insight, self-acceptance and learn to love ourselves in the higher realms, new possibilities are truly endless.

In the higher consciousness we develop the art of expecting the best of possibilities.

- To understand the higher conscious levels gives the spirit and the mind awesome power. It moves our entire being.
- Do not judge yourself. Evaluate, clean up your act and always move upward.
- Do not judge yourself through the "eyes" of others for they know not. Grow into your real self by detachment from all junk.
- Develop your power of discernment for in it you will "see" truth. A must for advancement.
- Go beyond your present beliefs for all are narrow now.
- Learn the constant process of positive thought = positive results.
- To become a good learner we must learn to accept not reject information.
- Virtues are the foundations of goodness.
- With love your whole world blossoms.
- The universe is friendly if only you knew.
- We were sent into the world to live.
- The greatest (sin) of all is an unlived life.
- Lead by a tender hand.
- Love with all your being.
- We need only to believe we can, to accomplish anything.
- Be of great -spirit, you will be great.
- **Conquer your world, the one within and you have conquered all.**

Inquisitive

Most folks seem satisfied
Just to get by.
That's just fine, but I want
To know why.
What's out there, what's up there
It can't be too high?
The mountains of life are mysterious
Just makes me want to try!

Keep on keeping on. Never give up, NEVER! You are already there. Image it; believe it!

GO IN LOVE & PEACE! RISE TO YOUR GREAT PLACE IN LIFE.

ADVANCE TO YOUR TRUE SELF!

The recipe of knowing how to advance to a higher spiritual level should be understood. The empowering virtues must now be reinstated into our being. Rise to your great place in life! No matter how large or small your task, it is very important. Do it well!!

VIRTUES

LIFE'S ENRICHMENTS

FOREWORD .... *Donald C. Decker*

Virtues empower you. They are the ingredients of our value system. Virtues structure principles and rules that build morality. Virtues are the keys to goodness and excellence both in individuals and society. Virtues are free, everybody can get them.

Do not be careless with your endowed virtues.

They are the tools of your high destiny. Knowing and practicing virtues will not make you perfect nor take away your fun. They are essential to your very health, happiness and wellness. There dwells in all of us a divine energy that is propelled by virtues.

Read and practice a virtue each day. Read aloud the affirmations in the boxes. Your life will be enriched. You will develop a new spiritual enthusiasm. Virtues develop spiritual health and well-being which supports total wellness; a balanced healthy person.

Do not judge yourself through someone else's eyes. Look into your own being and see your potential. Work on it. The greatest virtue of all life's achievements is victory over oneself. Those who know this victory can never really know defeat.

Faith is seeking and believing - trust is faith. Faith is empowered by listening and knowing. Hearing and seeing brings faith. Trust and faith in oneself is the first step toward any success. Hearing through an open ear brings our sensory mechanisms information. A closed ear shuts out the world of learning. Hearing helps develop knowledge. Understanding brings truth. Truth brings trust and faith. Faith is seeking universal Reality through the Divine Creator.

Patience is an equanimity that enables us to rise superior to the trials and tribulations of life.

Love is the absolute power behind all goodness. The human condition that is exemplified by unconditional love has the ability to ascend to the perfection of universal love and consciousness. This is the essence of life. This is the path to peace and true knowledge. Finding the Divine Source of all things is the true purpose of life. All the rest is sheer illusion of Reality and will last but a brief moment in the importance of life. No one needs to judge you, for you will lay down your own path directed by your own will. There is no outside influence that keeps you from the spiritual path of goodness, for both love and hate are available for your own choosing. There is a perfect answer, a positive solution to all problems by the application of love and spiritual know how!

Our deepest fear is not that we are inadequate. Our deepest fear is that we are powerful beyond measure. It is our light, not our darkness, that most frightens us. We ask ourselves, who am I to be brilliant, talented and noble? Actually who are we not to be this and more?

<u>You are a child of the great Creation</u>. Playing small does not serve the world. There is nothing enlightened about shrinking so that other people won't feel insecure around you. We were born to make manifest the glory of God that is within us. It's not just in some of us, it is in everyone! As we let our own light shine, we unconsciously give other people permission to do the same. As we are liberated from our own fear, our presence naturally liberates others. Fear cannot abide where there is love for they are opposites and cannot take up the same space at the same time. Love is wellness, while fear destroys our very existence. You must realize that the real you is love and you are expected to perform in a noble and loving manner. That is your main calling.

The first step in learning is found in acceptance, not rejection. Rejection and prejudice stop the real process of learning and taking into your bio-computer (brain) of information and fact.

Ignorant rejection of proper consideration of new information keeps one in the darkness of ignorance. Those who do not understand the process of discernment rarely learn or advance much in a lifetime.

First we must take the information into our spiritual and mental organizer, our soul and bio-computer. We study it without pre-judgment, give it the possibilities of truth and fact. It is important we go beyond our present sense of it. Investigate it, add the accepted facts to our discerning spiritual and mental capabilities. Process the new information, accepting new possibilities and discarding the junk through discernment. We must learn to add to our valuable knowledge base on a daily basis.

This is a process of personal growth by the power of knowledge and a new openness to wider thought. The world is vast. Even if we make a grand effort to know its great secrets we shall never know but a drop in the ocean of knowledge and wisdom. Why most are satisfied with barely a molecule I am not sure. It is all so exciting!

Learning spiritual facts is the greatest way to the fullness of life. I offer you these great bits of knowledge and wisdom. These truths are universal in nature and have always been out in the universe and on occasion been taken in by man as true knowledge.

INTRODUCTION

Virtue is a spiritual conformity of right, moral excellence.

Human happiness and progress are founded on spiritual knowledge and behavior. In the near future, the masses will reawaken to their spiritual beings.

Virtues are the spiritual building blocks and recognition of the good in all of us. Virtues empower values and morality. They are the link of body and mind to spirit. Virtues are the eternal signs of the right behavior of human kind. Without the subconscious and conscious awareness of virtues, humankind has the distinct ability to act out in irrational and barbaric behavior. Without the knowledge and action of these essential building blocks of a positive life, we can destroy ourselves and the civilization around us.

Virtues are the cornerstones of great people and societies. Virtues consist of the spiritual character and behavior of individuals, institutions, and all segments of society. The great societies of the world have risen when virtues have empowered their people. When these virtues are removed from a society, the negative aspects of greed, ignorance, unrestrained criminal activities, and man's inhumanity to man destroys that civilization.

Many times the destruction of a glorious society took place so slowly the people did not see or recognize the destructive elements. More often, however, they saw the decay all around them and chose to be part of the silent majority. They became part of the lethargic, apathetic population that stood by while the greatness of their country fell around them into nothingness and was no more!

When virtues no longer hold a society together, it falls into decay. The very institutions that once gave it meaning become dysfunctional and actually assist in the cause and effect of its destruction.

"America the beautiful, God shed His grace on thee and crowned thy good with brotherhood from sea to shining sea." This great nation is presently in a free fall downward. This land, especially endowed by its Creator, is in serious trouble. The institutions of law, education, medicine, and business are suffering from the lack of virtue empowerment. People of insight recognize this truth. We are a nation that has lost its integrity.

As a society, we have already looked under a thousand rocks for solutions to the problems caused by these dysfunctional social systems. The statistics and our social behavior prove no empowering solution has yet been found for this increasing social cancer that has invaded our present society.

No institution of the United States has been able to reverse the negative aspects of a decaying society. The perceived solutions are part of a transformation, but they address only small pieces of a bigger problem. The solution to this national dilemma is not expensive. It is quite simple if administered properly by caring people who are not prejudiced.

We have learned through experience that money is not the answer. Our behavior and its resulting statistics prove that fact.

First, we must become aware of the void of virtuous behavior. We fail to recognize what virtues are and how they contribute to basic harmony. Our lack of understanding makes us apathetic and our demeanor suggests that we either do not care or are at a loss as to what to do. **We feel we cannot make a positive difference, so we become part of the silent majority that, by silence, kills a nation.**

If we are to develop our spiritual knowledge and look to a bright future for our country, we must establish or re-establish virtues. This can now be done by introducing to our citizens specific courses designed to focus on the art and understanding of virtuous living.

We cannot build enough prisons to hold the criminal element if we refuse to install virtues in our every day life. We cannot improve our schools until we put virtues into a daily curriculum. We cannot change government for the better until we install virtues into all its activities. We cannot improve the effectiveness of our justice system until we reinstate virtues. We cannot improve the effectiveness and efficiencies of our economy without the reinstatement of virtues, values, principles, and morality. We cannot develop the higher aims of humanity toward a harmonious, loving society without hatred, prejudice, rape, murder, theft, and abuses of all kinds until we diligently reintroduce and empower the population with virtues.

We must instill in the minds and spirit of our fellow citizens the high aims and expectations of a virtuous society. We cannot expect to produce a safer, peaceful, joyous society until virtues become a wonderful teaching to all of our citizens. When we refuse to become virtue smart we enable a society to decay.

We will not be able to cause friendliness, kindness, and understanding to be part of our society until we, with all the power at hand, put virtuous knowledge into the being of our people. No person or nation can, without the knowledge, understanding, and positive behaviors that results from a virtuous society made up of people like you and me, in the love and practice of virtues.

It has been said through all the ages from the being of Isaiah to Socrates. "My people destroy themselves because they reject knowledge and virtue."

I am going to venture that human kind is now meditating on life and its true meaning. We are starting to accept the kinship of all people acknowledging unity with man and the universe. We are infusing into our being the true essence of creation and civilization. We are yearning to know and understand our innate virtues. We are learning that the integration of life and virtues leads to the balance of inner thought and positive outward behavior. This results in personal and social integrity.

A transformation of the individual and society takes place when virtues are enacted. We can put these truths within your reach, but it is your responsibility to take this knowledge and enrich your life.

Your understanding of virtues is key to a productive life. They bring happiness and peace. They bring you knowledge. The words in this book will empower your life. Practice virtues!

ORIENTATION

The time has come for society in all its' segments to understand the reality of virtues. Virtues are the foundation for values, principles and morality. The combination of these essential ingredients of life bring harmony and stability to the individual and to society at large.

Before we allow further deterioration of our society, we must address the reasons for its cause. It should be understood that these priceless guidelines to civilized living were not "invented". There have always been universal laws, the very foundations that lead to good health. They are part of our human conditions and spiritual soundness that develops positive thinking patterns. To the degree people recognize and live in harmony with virtuous principles they act and grow in a productive manner.

When the behavior patterns and knowledge of virtues are missing, the individual self-destructs and society disintegrates. The reinstatement and teaching of virtues is essential, or we are all lost!

Although the tendency to engage in virtuous behavior is probably innate in each of us, it can be easily squashed in a child. Many people are reared in environments - homes and neighborhoods - which, by example, misdirect our behavior. Therefore, virtuous living must be taught and consistently reinforced by as many social institutions as possible. Today there seems to be confusion concerning these universal laws. Be it known that universal laws transcend all boundaries and opinions. They are not only world-wide, encompassing all people, they are also eternal.

Every home, civic organization, and educational institution should teach virtues. The natural growth toward an acceptable value system comes from virtue knowledge and recognition. Until this basic education is established and taught, our nation will continue to be extremely problematic. We will not be able to clean up our act.

Universal laws pervade all things; they also sustain all things. We can no longer deny ourselves of the tremendous benefits of teaching ethical behavior. If we continue without this empowerment, we shall suffer more. History has taught us that mankind has the distinct ability to act out irrational and barbaric behaviors.

On the other hand, we know that man has risen also to great heights when directed from negative to positive influences. So, we must regard humankind as a gem of unestimatible value. Education can bring out and reveal our human treasures, and enable people to benefit from them. These laws can reduce the dissensions that divide us and cause prejudice and violence.

Universal laws succeed where civil laws fail. The proper education of people of all ages is of vital importance. We should know by now that a value system is necessary. At this time, the primary and most urgent requirement is the promotion of education. It is inconceivable that any person or nation should achieve continued success without this fundamental concern being addressed and carried forward.

The simple recognition that humankind is now searching for a higher consciousness is proof that society and its' institutions need to provide this knowledge. Virtues are the ingredients that will mobilize the enthusiasm for a better society. The virtues explained in this text are the building blocks of life itself. Without the empowerment of values, principles, and morality, we are extremely limited. With this knowledge we can create our own positive future.

Virtues are indeed the link of body and mind to the largest and most important aspect of the human being: our spirituality. Virtues are the internal spiritual qualities that cause the positive external signs and actions of right behavior in people.

When we finally understand the power of universal laws, our world citizens will grow into a harmonious maturity. The natural progression of our species is at the threshold of harmony and peace. In order to make this quantum leap, universal laws, as pertaining to the human condition, must be taught and understood. A basic virtues curriculum must be established at every level of education. Until we do this, we will continue in this barbaric adolescent state that is controlling human behavior.

The knowledge on virtues in this text should bring growth into the life of the student. It emphasizes the importance of self-worth so we can be all we are created to be. The knowledge of virtues contributes to our ability to be useful citizens for the betterment of our world.

We should see that the degradation of humankind that has persisted though centuries must cease. Humankind must now replace the idea of oppression and killing with the idea of cooperative co-existence. Every person must stop thinking of life as some battle or conquest to be won by force, but rather as important work to be done together. This is the day of knowledge when we shall come to understand truth and reality. The loving tenacity and human perseverance for the betterment of our society will become premier in the hearts, minds and consciousness of all the people of the world.

For you my friend: Knowledge is as wings to peoples' lives, and a ladder for their ascent. In truth, the universal laws of virtues are a tremendous treasure for all of us and a source of glory, of bounty, of joy, of exaltation, of growth, of cheer and of gladness. The heedless will suffer. Take your choice!

WORDS

My inspiration for words of life
    Comes on occasion from the depths of strife.
Not so much from mind and tongue
    But from my breath and soul undone.
The pain of life is worth the trip
    For my emotion needs put to script.
Without written word or records mood
    No one but God knew where I stood.
My love and yearning would never be known
    No one on earth could know I've grown.
Without the power of words to tell
    The inmost secrets of my life do dwell.
For in the quiet of my creative mind
    I can expose the wonderment of humankind,
Can allow the deepest thoughts to dwell,
    And put them down in words that tell.

Donald C. Decker

INDEX

**Virtues are universal laws.
They are innate and equal divine perfection.**

Assertiveness	149
Caring	151
Character	153
Class	155
Cleanliness	157
Compassion	159
Confidence	161
Consideration	165
Cooperation	167
Courage	171
Courtesy	173
Creativity	175
Detachment	179
Determination	183
Discernment	187
Empathy	190
Enthusiasm	192
Excellence	194
Faithfulness	198
Flexibility	202
Forgiveness	206
Friendliness	210
Generosity	212
Gentleness	214
Giving	216
Goodness	218
Gratitude	220
Helpfulness	222

Honesty	224
Honorableness	226
Humility	228
Idealism	230
Integrity	234
Joyfulness	236
Justice	238
Kindness	240
Love	242
Loyalty	246
Mercy	248
Moderation	250
Modesty	254
Obedience	256
Orderly	259
Patience	261
Peacefulness	265
Prayerfulness	269
Purpose	273
Reliability	276
Respect	278
Responsibility	282
Reverence	284
Self-Discipline	287
Sincerity	289
Spirituality	291
Steadfastness	295
Tactfulness	297
Tolerance	301
Trust	304
Trustworthiness	306
Truthfulness	308
Understanding	311

Truth
Is violated by
Falsehoods
It is outraged by
Silence
But, it is killed by
DENIAL...
This is the absolute
Time for truth!

VIRTUES: Life's Enrichments

Assertiveness

Assertive is to be positive and confident.

When you are assertive you are aware that you are a worthy person. You know you have your own special gifts. You have a healthy self-esteem and recognize your unique combination of qualities.

You will gain the respect of others when you excel in kindly assertiveness. When you are assertive, you don't follow others. You think for yourself. You are confident so you don't act in an overbearing way, you are just positively assertive. You express your own ideas, opinions and talents. When you are assertive you serve your family, job and the world around you in your own special way.

A person that is not assertive is passive. We would not be our own person if we were passive. We would just blow in the wind and become non-productive. When we lack assertive confidence, we just react to the things other people demand of us. If we are excessively passive, we allow others to hurt us or lead us into trouble. We do not set limits that keep us safe. The trouble with being too passive is that your special way of being and thinking would remain unexpressed and the world would be a poorer place; that would be quite a loss.

Be assertive, but not aggressive. Do not try to control other people by any type of aggression - just be assertive. When you are assertive, others respect you. You are offering your true ideas and feelings as well as protecting yourself. When you are assertive you choose what you will do for reasons of your own.

You stand up for what you know is right. You are your own leader. When someone suggests something you know is wrong, tell them you will not do it; be assertive. You are actually here as a blessing to the world. Share your true feelings. Do what is right - assert your positive self.

I will refuse to react to others without thinking or finding out how I really feel about things first. My renewed self-confidence will allow the virtue of assertiveness to become a daily part of my life. I will think and learn for myself & I will be assertive.

CARING

Caring is giving love & attention to people and things.

Caring about other people is absolutely essential to a happy life. When you care for someone, you pay a lot of attention to them and take an interest in what is happening to them. You can show you care about someone by saying and doing things that help them. Caring about something you are doing means giving it your best. When you care about something you treat it gently and respectfully.

You can care for yourself, for others, for an animal or a special thing. Caring about other people is part of the necessity of following the Golden Rule, "Do unto others as you would have them do unto you". Caring about yourself means that you treat yourself with the respect and concern that you deserve. And when you care for an animal, you watch over it and take good care of its needs.

Without caring, nothing and no one really matters. Without caring people would only do things for others because they expect something in return. When people have an attitude of "I don't care", they do sloppy or incomplete work. When you don't care others get the impression that you don't matter much. They start being careless too.

Caring comes from within. Caring is a sign of love, respect and concern. Caring people take the interest of others as their own. They do all they can to show people that they are loved and valued. When you are a caring person, you handle things with control and gentleness. When someone or something is entrusted to your care, you treat their trust as something special, giving nothing but your best. When you care about yourself, you treat your body with respect, you take care of your needs, you seek knowledge and you naturally become a peaceful, productive citizen.

ONE OF THE ESSENTIAL VIRTUES THAT ALLOWS YOU TO SOAR WITH EAGLES IS A CARING HEART. YOU CANNOT FLY WITHOUT THIS VIRTUE - CARING.

Character

A good character is the essence of many virtues, moral excellence, and firmness.

Character is the complex combination of mental and ethical traits making and marking a person as an individual. It tells us of the attributes or features that make up and distinguish the individual. It is the detectable expression of the individual character that makes us wonderfully different. To have good character means we have moral understanding and principles of high level. The character of a person is very important.

The characteristics of a person give us a sketch of the qualities of a particular social type of that individual. We should constantly strive to develop good character by practicing virtues and virtuous behaviors. Our characteristics are distinctive qualities that indicate our special identity. It's a very important part of life. We should remember that our characteristics are utilized to distinguish the person. It is important that we develop our precious individuality. We should always remember that in developing honorable character, we do not hurt others nor do we say negative things about other people.

We should strive to develop the interesting individual that we are. We are indeed a one-of-a-kind, the wonderful, singular, and unique being created by God and your parents. We should remember in the gift of life we have been given distinctive qualities that distinguish us from others. In true recognition that difference is a wonderful thing. We must remember that all people have their own genius, their own distinction, their own superior and inferior capabilities, but they are all praiseworthy when they have a goodly character.

Today we should express these wonderful characteristics of our personality and of our being. We should not become part of the flock of sheep that travels down a blind, boring path together. As individuals, we have distinct characteristics, we should be proud of them.

I WILL WORK DAILY TO DEVELOP THE WONDERFUL CHARACTER OF MY DIVINE GREATNESS. I WILL RID MYSELF OF THE NEGATIVE THOUGHTS OF MY OWN CHARACTER AND BRING INTO ACTION THE WONDERFUL PERSON I WAS INTENDED TO BE. I HAVE GOOD CHARACTER. MY CHARACTER WILL BE EMPOWERED BY LEARNING AND BEHAVING IN A VIRTUOUS MANNER.

Class

Class is the virtue of good manners and stability.

Class never runs scared. It is sure footed and confident in the knowledge that you can meet life head on and handle whatever comes along. Class always shows spiritual strength.

Those who have class can wrestle with their own internal problems or life's outward problems and win the victories with humble dignity. Class never makes excuses. It takes it's lumps and learns from past mistakes. Class is considerate of others at all times. It knows that good manners are nothing more than wonderful small sacrifices.

Class has no boundaries of ancestry or money. The most affluent blue blood can be without class, while the poorest may show class in every act of life. Class never tries to build itself up by tearing others down or by boasting. Class is already up and need not strive to look better by making others look worse. Class is humble confidence, it can walk with kings and keep it's virtue and talk with crowds and keep the common touch.

Class is a very important virtue. It assists with getting along with many types of people. Everyone seems comfortable with the person who has class because they are comfortable with themselves.

> **WHEN WE HAVE CLASS WE ARE BEYOND PREJUDICE. PEOPLE WITH CLASS HELP CREATE COMFORTABLE AND PEACEFUL SURROUNDINGS. EACH OF US HAS THE ABILITY OF CLASS; LET'S DEVELOP IT.**

Cleanliness

Cleanliness means keeping your body clean; practicing cleanliness everywhere.

When you practice cleanliness you feel fresh. Cleanliness means keeping your room neat and clean. It means doing your share to help your family to keep your home and your surroundings in order.

Cleanliness can be in your mind as well as your body. A clean mind means that you keep your thoughts on things which are good for you. You can clean up your act by deciding to change when you have done something you aren't proud of or when you have made a mistake. Cleaning is like wiping the slate clean and starting over when you want to improve yourself.

Staying clean, can also mean keeping your body free of harmful substances, such as drugs or alcohol. In every aspect of life, purity, cleanliness and refinement exalt the human condition and further your development. Cleanliness produces a healthy thought and attitude condition. Cleanliness also shows respect for others. It makes you nice to be around. Cleanliness is extremely important because it protects you from disease.

Being willing to clean things up in your behavior, to fix your mistakes, makes you happy inside. When you keep yourself and your surroundings clean, it makes your spirit strong, peaceful and confident.

Cleanliness means to remove disarray and things that interfere with your well being. Cleanliness is about clean language. It's about clean thought. When unpleasant thoughts are on our mind, we must replace them with thoughts that are good for us.

WE MUST EXAMINE FOR CLEANLINESS BOTH OUTSIDE THE BODY AND WITHIN. TODAY YOU SHOULD START TO KEEP YOURSELF FRESH AND CLEAN. YOU SHOULD MAKE A SPECIAL EFFORT TO PUT YOUR THINGS IN YOUR LIFE IN ORDER FOR THE BENEFIT OF SELF AND OTHERS AROUND YOU. LET'S CLEAN UP OUR ACT.

COMPASSION

Compassion is understanding and caring about someone else.

Compassion is one of the most highly regarded virtues. Compassion is understanding and caring about someone who is in trouble or who has made a mistake. It is being kind and forgiving. It is feeling sorry when someone is hurt and needs someone to understand. We are compassionate because we now know we could be that person that is hurt or has made a mistake. It is forgiving someone who hurt you because you understand this can happen directly or indirectly.

In compassion we feel the pain of someone who is in trouble even if you do not know that person. It is caring deeply and wanting to help even if all you can do is to say kind words. Compassion is a mature thing to have. It is a sign of the growing up of a person spiritually dedicated to the love and understanding of other people.

When people feel bad or find themselves in trouble they usually feel very much alone. Feeling alone at times like these can make things even worse. At such times as these, people start to believe that no one understands or cares about them at all. Being compassionate tells the person that they are not alone. It makes you a friend when someone needs a friend. It gives you a good feeling and makes you useful at the same time. Try to seek out people in your life that may need your compassion. This is a great step in your own maturity. Compassion helps you to understand other people and yourself.

Without compassion, the world is a hard and lonely place. With compassion, we are all connected and hard times are much easier to bear because others understand and care. With compassion it is a kindly world. It is a world of supporting each other and looking in when others need help. Compassion is a great virtue.

COMPASSION WILL MAKE GREAT FRIENDSHIPS BECAUSE PEOPLE LOVE TO BE UNDERSTOOD. THEY LOVE THE ATTENTION OF ANOTHER HUMAN BEING. WE SHOULD ALWAYS ACT WITH COMPASSION.

Confidence

Confidence is being certain and feeling assured.

Confidence carries great rewards; it comes from knowing and trusting. Self confidence means you trust yourself. You can do things without doubts holding you back. You know your own strengths and weaknesses. These knowing conditions of self produce that confidence to continue courageously.

When you are confident in others, you rely on them and trust them. Confidence in our fellow man is very important, however we must learn to pick and choose through discernment those people to trust. Confidence in your self is a sense of trust that your Creator and parents did not make a mistake. You are loved. They watch over you as you go through life. Confidence brings peace of mind. You are confident, you act with strength. You like to try new things. Confidence means that you don't allow fear or doubt to keep you from doing what you really want to do and directs you towards successful goals that bring great rewards.

With confidence, you feel certainty even when others try to confuse you or make you doubt. You do your best without worrying about what is going to happen. Worry is not a part of the confident person's life. Instead of being afraid of failure, you have confidence that you can learn. If you lack confidence you will miss a lot because your fear of making a mistake is great. We must remember that making mistakes is a part of everyone's life. It doesn't mean that you are not worthwhile. Mistakes are the stepping stones to a better place - to a higher confidence. Confidence in your own being replaces worry and fear. Confidence gives you the ability to try new things and fail sometimes. We were brought into this world not to show off how perfect we are but to learn to improve ourselves step by step.

You practice confidence by knowing that you are worthwhile whether you win or lose - succeed or fail. You see yourself as a learner and you welcome new experiences and new possibilities. You watch yourself without judging. You don't criticize yourself harshly.

BECAUSE I HAVE SELF CONFIDENCE I CAN TRY SOMETHING NEW AND GIVE IT MY BEST EFFORT. I CAN LEARN FROM MY MISTAKES. I AM FREE FROM WORRY. I WELCOME NEW POSSIBILITIES AND TRUST MY WILL AND CHOICES TO SUPPORT ME IN ALL MY ENDEAVORS. IF I TRULY KNOW MYSELF I WILL HAVE THE CONFIDENCE TO SUCCEED! KNOW THYSELF FOR YOU ARE EXTREMELY CAPABLE, IF YOU ONLY KNEW!

Personal Virtues Score Card

Score for virtues before virtues lessons.
Virtues 1-10   Be your own judge!

Assertiveness _____
Care _____
Character _____
Class _____
Cleanliness _____
Compassion _____
Confidence _____
Consideration _____
Cooperation _____
Courage _____
Courtesy _____
Creativity _____
Detachment _____
Determination _____
Discernment _____
Empathy _____
Enthusiasm _____
Excellence _____
Faithfulness _____
Flexibility _____
Forgiveness _____
Friendliness _____
Generosity _____
Gentleness _____
Giving _____
Goodness _____
Gratitude _____
Helpfulness _____

Honesty _____
Honorableness _____
Humility _____
Idealism _____
Integrity _____
Joyfulness _____
Justice _____
Kindness _____
Love _____
Loyalty _____
Mercy _____
Moderation _____
Modesty _____
Obedience _____
Orderliness _____
Patience _____
Peacefulness _____
Prayerfulness _____
Purpose _____
Reliability _____
Respect _____
Responsibility _____
Reverence _____
Self-Discipline _____
Sincerity _____
Spirituality _____
Steadfastness _____
Tactfulness _____
Tolerance _____
Trust _____
Trustworthiness _____
Truthfulness _____
Understanding _____

Consideration

Consideration is having regard for other people and their feelings.

People should always concern themselves with doing a kindly thing for their fellow man; offering someone love, consideration and thoughtful help. Consideration is thinking about how your actions will affect others and caring about how they might feel. Consideration is thoughtfulness. It is paying attention to what other people like and don't like, then doing things that give them happiness. Consideration is giving the same importance to others' likes and dislikes as you do to your own. When you have different tastes, consideration means you don't try to convince other people that they are wrong and you are right. You respect their needs and feelings. Consideration is doing things in a way that benefits others as well as yourself.

When we behave selfishly and don't practice consideration, we hurt people's feelings. When we are inconsiderate, others tend to be inconsiderate too. Let us not be selfish or inconsiderate. It upsets people and causes dissension in your life and to the people around you. Without consideration, people get into arguments because they feel their needs are being ignored. When we are considerate, things are more peaceful.

Consideration begins by noticing how your actions are affecting other people. Consideration is asking yourself things like "will this hurt or disturb someone else?" A considerate person respects other people's rights. To be considerate, give some thought to what would bring another happiness. When someone is ill, give them loving attention. If someone is sad, put yourself in their position and think about what you would need from a friend.

IF WE WOULD APPRECIATE HAVING OTHER PEOPLE BE CONSIDERATE TO US WE MUST BE CONSIDERATE OF OTHERS. YOU MUST THINK ABOUT THEIR FEELINGS AND NEEDS AS WELL AS YOUR OWN. WE MUST DO THOUGHTFUL THINGS WHICH BRING OTHER PEOPLE HAPPINESS. THIS IS THE POWER OF CONSIDERATION.

Cooperation

Cooperation is working with others to achieve a common goal or purpose.

Nobody can live without cooperation. The elements of cooperation consist of listening to each other, respecting each other's views and opinions, caring about the way goals are reached, and the cooperative attitude of goal reaching. In cooperation, we should always attack the work or problem at hand and not each other. When we work in cooperation, it is done in harmony that makes everyone comfortable. Cooperation is when two people or more work together and make what they are working on work. Cooperation is also when you care about what you are doing. Imagine how hard and confusing it would be if there were not cooperation.

In the world of disharmony and selfishness, one of the most important virtues of healing is cooperation. One of the best ways to see the benefits of cooperation of learning is cooperative working and cooperative living. It is to see how different it feels from other non-cooperative ways of working and learning. Cooperation is important from your individual walk of life, to sports, to government, to the corporate world and of course, cooperation across all borders in the world.

Cooperation today is one of the most important virtuous activities that can take place. International or global cooperation is essential to the continued development of the exchange of knowledge, of data and information in the world, to world peace.

Those who develop an attitude and a behavior of cooperation will become a part of the wonderful advancement of all peoples. Cooperation is an essential virtue, from the family to the governments to society at large. Cooperation is the virtue that allows justice and harmony and peace to become a reality.

The basic ingredients of cooperation consist of communication, consideration, collaboration, and compromise. These equal cooperation, which gives us a grand finale of goals and progress. It has been said that to communicate is the beginning of understanding. Understanding is where co-operation begins. In communication, we develop the harmonies of all relationships from individual, family, school, work, city, state, nation, and the world. After communication comes consideration, which has to do with the Golden Rule. Be thoughtful of other people's feelings. Be kind. Do unto them as you would have them do unto you. Be considerate and show respect. Remember, consideration is a great virtue. A cooperative person shows respect and, therefore, brings effectiveness and knowledge into their own life.

Another ingredient of cooperation is to collaborate, to work together in preparing something or some project. The next component of importance in cooperation is to compromise. Sometimes we have to give up a little of our own idea to reach a better overall goal where the sum of the parts are greater than the individual pieces. Compromise is a way to settle an argument or dispute by which each side agrees to give up a part of what it wants. We find that cooperation is an important aspect of any advancing, learning, or better result condition.

We should remember that conflict is one kind of negative interaction between people, and seldom if ever, has good results. Compromise and cooperation is one kind of positive interaction that will, most of the time, bring a positive harmonious result.

I WILL BE A COOPERATIVE PERSON. WHEN YOU COOPERATE, YOU LEARN NOT ONLY WHAT YOU ARE SUPPOSED TO DO, BUT YOU ALSO LEARN ABOUT THE PEOPLE YOU ARE WORKING WITH. COOPERATION IS A PERSONAL SKILL THAT CAN TAKE ME FAR IN ANY ENDEAVOR I SET OUT TO DO. I WILL COOPERATE FOR THE GREATER COMMON GOOD.

- *The freedom of the captive is hope.*

- *The major waste of life lies in the love we have not given.*

- *The soul is the essential part of a human being, it does not perish.*

- *Goodness never fails.*

Courage

Courage is personal bravery in the face of fear.

Courage is going ahead even when you feel like giving up or quitting. It is doing what needs to be done even when it is really hard or sometimes scary. Courage means recognizing a danger and standing firm. It doesn't mean taking unnecessary chances just to look brave. Courage is needed in trying new things, in facing difficult situations, and in picking yourself up after a mistake and trying again. It is doing what you know is right even if other people laugh at you or disbelieve in you.

Courage is a quality of the heart, the spirit of human kind. It comes from what you feel in your heart rather than just what you think. It comes from knowing yourself and knowing down deep that you can and should do something. Courage comes from knowing that God is there to help and that you can count on Him always. It is also believing in yourself.

Love can give us courage. It gives us strength and helps us to do the right thing without letting our fears stop us. Courage is the best thing you can have when you are scared or unsure. There are times when you are not sure that you can do something. You might feel alone, facing what seems to be an impossible situation.

Courage helps you do great things. Without courage one would do only what is easy. No one would try new things that seem hard. When you are courageous, you do what you know is right even if society disagrees. You face your mistakes, you admit them, you learn from them and you keep trying. When you practice courage, you face all mistakes and life with this heartfelt confidence. You work to understand something which you were afraid of and decide if it is real or just imagined.

When you feel afraid, go ahead and feel your fear, then let it go. My friend, in the process of life, those who become fulfilled, accomplished and happy have courage in their heart.

COURAGE IS THE HEARTFELT ABILITY TO CARRY OUT YOUR CONVICTION NO MATTER WHAT. I AM BRAVE ENOUGH TO ADMIT MY MISTAKES. I HAVE THE COURAGE TO DO WHAT I KNOW IN MY HEART IS RIGHT.

Courtesy

Courtesy is to be polite, considerate and have gracious ways.

Courtesy is the prince of virtues. Courtesy is a way of acting and behaving with people which makes them feel valued, cared for and respected. It is important to practice courtesy with all people, friends and relatives, not just people we are meeting for the first time. You should use courteous expressions which let people know you appreciate them, are glad to see them and care about their feelings. Courtesy is one of the finest virtues that we can use to show respect for others.

Courtesy also means to think of how your behavior and your words are affecting others and then be sensitive to do things properly so that they are comfortable. It is necessary when being courteous to use the proper words. "Please" and "thank you" are ones we know quite well. However every word spoken should be considered with regard to how kindly and courteously they may affect other people.

When a person doesn't practice courtesy, people feel insulted and assume that the person is ignorant. They get the impression the person just doesn't care about anyone or anything. Rude people are avoided because others don't feel appreciated. They feel insulted and want to stay away from you.

Practicing courtesy makes every person feel important and acknowledged. No one feels taken advantage of or insulted. A courteous person develops proper relationships and self-confidence.

A person who extends courtesy, day by day, increases their self-esteem. If you are courteous, each time people come in contact with you they enjoy being around you and want to help you.

COURTESY IS LIKE A MAGNET - IT MAKES YOU ATTRACTIVE TO OTHERS. PRACTICING COURTESY EMPOWERS YOU AND MAKES OTHERS FEEL COMFORTABLE AROUND YOU. COURTESY IS ESSENTIAL FOR THE MUTUAL GROWTH OF RESPECT. PRACTICE DAILY - COURTESY.

CREATIVITY

Creativity means to bring something new into being.

You are a new creation. No one has ever been born who is exactly like you. You are expressing new ideas and inventions, new kinds of music, dance or art. It is a way to let the light of originality within you shine out for the benefit of others.

Creativity connects us with beauty. Creativity is anything that leads to improvement. Creativity can be expressed in an idea that may never have been expressed before. It is also seeing old things in a different light, with your special combination of gifts and talents. You were given these gifts. Creativity is a way to use them to bring new things into the world. Creativity is a way to use the spark new ways, doing things in a way that has not been done before.

Creativity is also the process of discovery. Through learning about science, you get the tools to discover the mysteries that Creation has placed in the world.

The best use of creativity is when you produce something that will benefit others. Creativity is sharing your special gifts.

Look at creativity as one of the most important virtues of humankind. Without creativity there would be no advancement in the world. Things would stay the same. Without great ideas, there would be no new inventions. We would just keep doing things as they have always been done. Boring! We would still be riding donkeys to get somewhere instead of taking plane, train, boat or car.

Creativity in one degree or another is part of the soul or virtuous condition of all beings. Creativity is most important for it brings about the finest in new ideas that produce a higher plane of consciousness for human life. We please our creator when we practice the gift of creativity in our lives.

We are the instruments of The Creator's human creativity. We all have different aspects, different ideas that mold our creative self. And we practice creativity by developing our gifts to the fullest. Each of us must find out what our creative gifts are by noticing what you like to do. Then learn how to develop your gifts and talents so that you get better at them.

Creativity is discipline in the service of vision. When you have a vision of something you want to create, you need to learn how to make it real. Creativity leads to an improvement. Practicing creativity means doing things your very own way.

Use knowledge and training to develop your gifts. Most importantly do things in your own unique way for you are a unique creation.

> CREATIVITY ADDS NEW THINGS TO LIFE. EACH ONE OF US MUST STRIVE TO BE CREATIVE, TO USE OUR SPECIAL GIFTS GOD GAVE US TO BRING BEAUTY AND ORIGINALITY INTO THE WORLD. WE MUST ALL THINK OF NEW AND BETTER WAYS TO DO THINGS.

- *Virtues values, principals and morality are the pillars of a productive life. They have been designed by the Creator. They are your foundations of strength.*

- *Do not sacrifice the spiritual for the material for one is wellness and eternal while the other will perish.*

- *Righteousness is the fulfillment of your creative purpose in every person's life. It develops a healthy soul.*

- *Your life gains purpose because of Divine Creation and your own efforts!*

Detachment

Detachment is experiencing your feelings without allowing your feelings to control you.

Detachment is one of the most empowering of all the virtues. It gives you the ability to choose what to do in a particular situation rather than having the situation dictate what you will do. Feelings like sadness, happiness, disappointment, joy, frustration and even anger are natural. Some of these emotions are lower level behavior, and some of them are behaviors found in the four higher spiritual conscious levels. Everyone has them.

Detachment is a spiritual quality that allows us to use thinking and feeling together, so that you don't let your feelings run away with you.

Detachment is a power of letting go of your past struggles. It allows choice of feelings. It frees us from negative emotions. Some people think detachment means being cold or pretending not to care, but when they try it, they find it is a joyful experience. Feelings are wonderful when they belong to us by choice, when we use them to do what we really want and choose to do.

Detachment means to feel what you feel but not have to act on the feeling unless you want to. Detachment is very important for a spiritual being. It allows you to choose the way you are going to act no matter how you feel. One of the strongest aspects of the art of detachment is that it permits you to be kind to people even those you do not like. Detachment helps you to decide what to do about strong feelings like anger. You can decide to use your voice to tell someone how mad you are and why. Or you can decide to lose your temper and pick up the nearest object to throw.

Detachment can help your self confidence. It is like going to a calm, peaceful place within your mind and looking at what is happening without getting swept away. Without detachment, you never know what you are going to do. It depends on how you feel! The more you practice detachment, the easier it becomes to do, even when your emotions are very strong. Praying and meditation can be a big help in learning detachment because it is a spiritual quality - a virtue.

Without detachment you will stay away from things that you don't like or are hard for you to do, even when it is very important for you to do them. With detachment you can choose to do something you like in moderation rather than neglecting other things that you need to do.

To recognize the feeling of the moment is the first step in learning to be detached. We must know what we are detaching from. Stop and look at your feelings and thoughts. Ask yourself what am I feeling about this? Then ask yourself what do I want to do, is it good for me, will it help someone else? When we are detached we see better. The final aspect and reward for learning detachment is that we can do what we decide to do with better results.

WE SHOULD ALWAYS BE AWARE OF OUR FEELINGS AND CHOOSE OUR ACTIONS WITH DETACHMENT. THEN WE CAN DO WHAT IS BEST FOR OURSELVES AND OTHERS. WE WILL THEN CHOOSE TO BE OUR BEST SELF NO MATTER WHAT HAPPENS. LET THE NEGATIVE PAST GO! DETACH!!

- We have been given tongues so we may say pleasant things to our fellow man.

- To increase your happiness forget the faults of others.

- Believe in today; each hour is precious.

- Make the best of today, for it is also your tomorrows, if you only knew.

DETERMINATION

Determination is using your willpower to do something even when it is really hard.

Determination is focusing your energies and efforts on a particular task and then sticking with what you are doing until the task is done. When you are determined you try and try, you work and work, until you get it done.

Determination means you care about doing something so much that even when it is really hard, you still keep going. You stay firm and on tract even when you are tested. You get help when you need help to go on. You don't stop until you are finished whether what you are doing will make a big difference or a little one. When you have decided to do something and you believe it is important, it gives you the feeling of great determination.

When you are encouraged to have determination, you will be able to accomplish many things in your life. People from their earliest years should have high aims and be taught to conduct themselves with determination. You should be firm in the purpose of your life. Without determination many things just don't get done, we put them off. When things get tough, people who are not determined just give up. They don't ask for help, even when they need it. They just stop. Without determination even important things get neglected.

When people are determined, even the hardest thing becomes a challenge they are willing to accept. They get things done. They grow stronger. Determined people do things which matter in the world. Most of them are not only determined for their personal accomplishments, they are also determined to help others.

A person developing determination must first decide what is important to them. Then they will use their willpower to make it happen. Determined people deal with obstacles in their way and then go back to what the major project is. One must keep going even if something starts to distract you. You must stay on the purpose of your project.

Determination is important for succeeding at anything, from learning to ride a bicycle to practicing the improvement of self. Determination is a powerful virtue. It is one of the most important aspects of reaching any goal that you should choose.

> WHEN ONE DEVELOPS DETERMINATION YOU MUST ALWAYS FINISH WHAT YOU START. THINK IT THROUGH FIRST, RECOGNIZE THE PROJECT OR GOAL, AND BEGIN WITH AN UNERRING, UNRELENTING DETERMINATION. WITH THIS POWERFUL TOOL YOU WILL ACCOMPLISH THE DREAMS AND THE GOALS OF YOUR LIFETIME.

- *Defamation or backbiting is only spoken by the ungodly.*

- *When virtues are practiced wellness comes.*

- *A bigot is blind & deaf and spiritually dead.*

- *A bigot prays, "my will be done." A spiritual seeker prays, "Thy will be done."*

DISCERNMENT

Discernment is keenness of insight and true perception of truth.

Discernment is a spiritual empowerment and a virtue that develops a keen sense of discriminating information. It develops a high level of skill in the discerning patterns that give us the wisdom of perception, penetration, insight, and acumen, which is a power to see what is not evident. It is a quiet spiritual insight. When we are discerning, we are looking for accuracy, especially in reading character or motives of a society, an organization, or an individual.

Discernment assesses the power within to distinguish and select what is true, factual, appropriate, or genuinely excellent. Discernment implies a quick and sympathetic conclusion.

A discerning person does not live by hearsay and innuendo, but has a searching mind that goes beyond what is obvious or superficial. When we have the virtue of insight, it empowers our ability to discern right from wrong, truth from error. Discernment takes away the abilities of half truths, false beliefs, and superstition.

We have been taught and it is true that we are not the judges of other human beings. However, there is a practical judgment that must take place in life if we are to learn, to grow, to become part of a positive society. Discernment is one of the great gifts. It allows us to know truth from fiction, it allows us to grow into the world of wisdom and knowledge and understanding.

Discernment is one of the supreme virtues of humanity. It is one of the four greatest gifts bestowed upon human kind by the Creator. When we strive to acknowledge the importance of discernment, it frees us from the bondage of self and ignorance and ritualistic behavior based on misbelief or superstition. We will soon acknowledge that the happiness of humanity is based on virtues, the commandments of a loving Creator that are delivered to our being through the process of discernment. It is one of the major tools that allows us to arise, to go forward, to strive with success, to advance in our progressive path, to become somebody, and to attain goals. We should all work toward the virtue of being a discerning person.

THE GREATEST GIFTS FROM OUR CREATOR ARE WISDOM, KNOWLEDGE, UNDERSTANDING AND DISCERNMENT. IN THE QUIET NOW I WILL CONCENTRATE ON LEARNING DISCERNMENT FOR THE SAKE OF TRUTH. TO EMPOWER THESE GREATEST GIFTS, WE WERE GIVEN A WONDERFUL INTELLECT TO OPERATE THEM.

EMPATHY

Empathy is the kind willingness to be in another's feelings to help.

Empathy is a very important virtue. It gives us the ability to look into another person's situation. We can do this because we are empathetic and have extreme caring for the well being of another person.

Empathy is the willingness to participate, be a part of the feelings or ideas of another person. A person that has empathy is kind and considerate. Empathy also shows us the best way to be helpful to others because we reach out to them and try to understand things from their position.

When we show empathy, we show many other virtues. Empathy is a very mature behavior because it brings about cooperation and caring. In a society where empathy and cooperation prevail, we find success. The opposite of empathy is indifference. When we do not exhibit empathy to our fellow human beings, the world becomes a place of indifference and coldness. We never develop a wonderful intimacy of cooperation and help that is the foundation of a stable individual or society.

Empathy is so important if we are to have a happy, harmonious life. Without empathy we never really know the other person. We know that caring is essential in developing relationships. Empathy is the key to knowing and caring about our friends and associates. A person who has empathy will let go of their self-importance and reach out to help other people. When we believe in ourselves and recognize that we are a precious, special individual, we will automatically be converted into a person who has empathy and display it in kind and caring ways.

When we have empathy, we also are a loving person. We care and love other people. Love empowers us to higher levels of capability.

EMPATHY IS THE BEGINNING OF TRUE UNDERSTANDING OF OUR FELLOW MAN. I WILL WORK DILIGENTLY ON MY SPIRITUAL, LOVING, CARING, AND KIND BEING. I WILL SHOW EMPATHY TO ALL THE PEOPLE I MEET.

ENTHUSIASM

Enthusiasm is doing something with zeal and eagerness.

Enthusiasm is doing things wholeheartedly. It's giving 100%. When you are enthusiastic you get behind something with all your being, because enthusiasm means the power of God within your own being. When you are enthusiastic, you are excited about something, you look forward to it. It's being cheerful and happy and powerfully positive. It is the major spiritual igniting of your innate capabilities.

Enthusiasm is ignited by it's having a positive attitude. It is a special way of doing things. It brings cheerfulness and joy to whatever you do and it ensures that you will give it your very best. Enthusiasm makes even the dullest job seem fun. When you approach a project or job with enthusiasm, you will enjoy doing it and look forward to your next project. The most important empowerment that enthusiasm brings you is its ability to create energy and drive - to climb mountains, to complete projects and to know what to do.

Everything becomes quite boring to a person or a situation that has no enthusiasm. When enthusiasm is not part of your being, you won't get things done as well. People without enthusiasm actually have an attitude problem and people do not necessarily want to be around them. When your enthusiasm is low, it depicts a lack of spiritual awareness.

Enthusiasm is powerfully catching. When you are enthusiastic, people around you get caught up in your excitement. You will find it easier to do your best because you have the energy and direction directly focused on your project or need. Since enthusiasm is an attitude, it comes from inside you. You become enthusiastic by positive thoughts of all things. When you show your feelings of enthusiasm, you give other people encouragement.

ENTHUSIASM IS THE GREATEST POWER YOU HAVE THATCREATES THE BRIGHT AND POSITIVE SIDE OF LIFE. ENTHUSIASM MEANS "GOD'S POWER WITHIN."

EXCELLENCE

Excellence is doing your very best.

When you are aiming for excellence doing your best means you do not stop at good enough, but push yourself to do all you can and get as much right as possible. In doing your best you learn all you can and do all you can to help yourself and others in everything you do. If you have problems or questions you do not quit or ignore them. Instead you investigate the truth or answer or you ask someone for help. Because we must constantly strive for excellence it becomes a virtuous path for all other aspects of our behavior.

When you do your very best at home you treat family members with special care, knowing that it really matters in how your home life performs. When you do your best at school it means paying attention because you do not want to miss a single thing to learn. It means that when you have an assignment of any kind, you do it until you get it right. Doing your best on a job is no different, you must constantly strive to perform at your highest level for the integrity of the job and the success for yourself and everyone around you. Excellence predicts a very fine efficiently and effectiveness in your job and in all endeavors in your life.

Excellence also has many other influences on your life. Doing your best helps you find out what talents you have, which special gifts the Creator gave you. Doing your best also helps you find out who you are and what you should do. Doing your best helps you develop your potential. It enables you to be all you can be. Excellence gives you the best opportunity to accomplish all that is possible for you because other people recognize your excellent behaviors and capabilities.

Doing your best will also enable you to make a positive difference in the world in which you live. One must realize that excellence takes hard work, it does not come easy but the rewards are great. First in the process of excellence we must pick something worth doing. We must choose something that is possible for us to do but that can be a little further advanced than what we are used to. In order to create excellence in our life, we must practice and practice, until you even surprise yourself in how well you are doing at a particular task.

The important aspect of excellence is to make a plan to have the volition and will, the enthusiasm to carry out the plan and then get it into action. Just do it. Get it going. Let's finish it. This is the process of excellence.

The absolute attitude that one must develop in the search of excellence is to do better than you ever have before. In every task, either those that are part of your past or those that are coming up in your future, we must strive for excellence.

> **EVERY DAY I WILL STRIVE TO BE THE BEST I CAN BE. I WILL PRACTICE EXCELLENCE IN ALL THAT I DO. EXCELLENCE ALLOWS US TO SOAR WITH EAGLES! EXCELLENCE MAKES THINGS BETTER!**

- *Plant your seed on good ground.*

- *Light your light, hold it high.*

- *Forgiveness is a must for spiritual growth and peace.*

- *Repentance is a virtue.*

FAITHFULNESS

Faithfulness is being true to someone or something.

Faithfulness is holding to what you believe is important no matter what happens. It is belief that stands up to the test of time. It is starting out on a path and staying on it no matter how many times you stop or get distracted. In faithfulness you stand firm no matter what. Faithfulness comes from really knowing and living what you believe, no matter what other people say and do. When you are faithful you can be counted on. Faithfulness is the essence of true trust. Your commitment regardless of what comes up is of absolute importance for you to do. But be flexible at the same time.

Faithfulness is especially needed when you have beliefs and principles that other people cannot see or understand and cannot be proven at the moment. If you are truly faithful to your beliefs such as belief in God, honesty or friendship, people will see those things reflected in your actions. When you are faithful, you make your ideas real. Faithfulness is a real important virtue. It gives us the foundation of beliefs.

Those who do not have faithfulness are probably not reliable because they believe something one day and something else the next.

They never know what to believe. This is a very confusing set of circumstances. When people are faithful, you know what they stand for and you can trust them. Faithfulness brings accomplishments because things get done regardless of distractions.

It is extremely important in faithfulness that we learn and question and find answers about our particular beliefs. As you grow in your beliefs you practice them as best you can in your life. Being faithful to the laws of God means that you keep praying and learning about different faiths and trusting it will teach you truth. If other people try to talk you out of it, use your own discernment. Listen to your inner self when things come up to test your faith. Faith is not really faith unless it is tested and stays strong. Your faith gets stronger when your beliefs are tested. It is extremely important that you seek the truth of your faith on a constant basis that allows you to grow and understand the universal condition of creation.

You must be faithful in your deeds. Being faithful means you always keep your promises. You only make agreements you can keep. You try really hard to practice what you say. To do a job faithfully means you do it with as much excellence and precision as you can and you do it on time. When you are faithful in relationships, you are loyal. You don't talk about someone behind their backs. If you are mad or hurt, you go to them and talk about it privately. You don't leave friends when a new one comes along. You develop a high regard for loyalty when you are faithful.

> IT IS IMPORTANT TO CONSTANTLY LEARN ABOUT YOUR BELIEFS. YOU SHOULD BE FAITHFUL. YOU HAVE THE RIGHT TO PRACTICE YOUR OWN BELIEFS AND SHOW THEM IN YOUR DAILY ACTIONS. IN FAITHFULNESS WE ARE LOYAL. WE MUST KEEP ALL RESPONSIBILITIES, FAITHFULLY.

- *Do not go through life fast asleep!*

- *Be one of grace. His grace is so abundant it cannot be calculated.*

- *If you demand separation from God you will not be able to seek grace.*

- *The universe has the same religion as man; harmony with its Creator.*

FLEXIBILITY

Flexibility is being open to the need for change.

It is said today that flexibility is one of the most important aspects of business. If we are not flexible in our business or in our lives, the people who are make the changes at the proper time and become more successful. As we know many unexpected things happen to us. We cannot control many of the influences that affect our life. When we are open to growth or when upsetting things happen, these are messages that we need to do things differently or improve ourselves in some way.

Flexibility gives us the tools to make these changes more easily. When we are not flexible difficulties can destroy our happiness or put us into an attitude that is defensive. When we look at difficulties as challenges then we can make these necessary changes that give us the advantage.

Being flexible means that we do not insist on having our own way. We are open to the opinions and feelings of other people. With flexibility you are more mature and are willing to change your mind. If something doesn't work, you try a new way. That's being flexible. One of the best aspects of flexibility is realizing that making changes is not losing anything, it is only that you are becoming better and growing.

It is very important that you learn flexibility; that you learn to adjust and adapt. You keep making positive changes. When you are open to change you can accomplish more. Instead of doing things the same old way, you think of new and better ways to do them.

When things get tough, flexible people bend and become stronger. They keep learning and growing. People who have a hard time being flexible keep doing things the same old way when new ways are needed. One must be very careful to not become rigid. When we are rigid and things don't go our way or when they don't happen as we expected we get angry and upset.

Flexibility begins by recognizing a need to change something in yourself or your surroundings. It could be how to get things accomplished or the need to acquire one of the virtues. If something is in the way or isn't working for you, this is probably a sign that there is a need for change. If something keeps going wrong in an area of your life, this may be a test which you need to accept and embrace. It could be teaching you what is next in your spiritual growth. One of the most important virtues for the development of growth is flexibility. We must learn from the hard times in our life, make the adjustments, be flexible. Some say they don't like surprises; those who are flexible can handle surprises.

> I WILL BECOME MORE FLEXIBLE. I AM WILLING TO CHANGE MYSELF FOR THE BETTER. I WILL LOOK FOR NEW WAYS TO DO THINGS. BEING FLEXIBLE ALLOWS ME TO GROW FASTER.

- *Thought should come before speech!*

- *Once I had riches, it was nothing. Now I have nothing and am finally rich.*

- *Mankind must now seek his true nature - PEACE.*

- *Happiness comes from things and happenings. <u>Joyfulness comes from the spirit.</u>*

Forgiveness

Forgiveness is overlooking the mistakes of others and loving them as much as before.

Everyone makes mistakes. Every mature person must be forgiving, for they are not without error. Forgiving does not mean that all of a sudden you do not feel hurt or that the wrong choice someone made was right. It means that you find it in your heart to give the person another chance.

It is important that we talk and communicate properly about these mistakes. Forgiveness means you do not punish people for what they have done even if they deserve it. **Forgiveness is one of the most noble of virtues**. It is also essential for the development of a harmonious environment. Regardless of which social structure, whether it be individual, family, institutional or federal, one must be forgiving.

You should even forgive yourself. You sometimes do things that you are sorry for and wish you hadn't done. Forgiving yourself means to stop punishing yourself or feeling hopeless because you did something wrong. It is moving ahead, ready to do things differently, with compassion for yourself and faith you can change for the better. It is important to know that we have the power of free will and choice. This means it is up to us to do good or bad, right or wrong. For many reasons people sometimes choose to do the wrong thing. Everyone does at one time or another. No matter what people do that aggravates you. Whether it be little or big we must be forgiving. It is important to us that people forgive us and are willing to let us try again.

If you are being forgiving of yourself you can learn from your mistakes. Forgiveness is the best way to encourage yourself to be better. We know it feels bad not to be forgiven. When people are not forgiving of us they don't give us a second chance. If you are not forgiving and kind about it, others will always be a little frightened around you. People will still make mistakes because they are human. But if we are not forgiving people lose hope and fall into despair. Forgiveness is an order of Creation.

One must not fool themselves and think you have forgiven someone but really still feel mad inside. If the forgiveness is not a loving act you will continue to punish yourself and the other person subconsciously. It is also important that you look upon the good things someone does because it will make it easier to forgive them when they do something wrong.

It is important to forgive everyone for those acts they have done against you. But it is especially important to forgive those you love for that love will overpower the feelings of hurt. God can place forgiveness in your heart if you have trouble forgiving. A person who is not forgiving carries the negative burden of un-forgiveness. Anguish in life!

FROM THIS DAY FORWARD I WILL BE FORGIVING TO MYSELF AND TO ALL OTHER PEOPLE. FORGIVENESS CLEARS THE WAY FOR BETTER RELATIONS IN OUR FUTURE. IT IS ESSENTIAL FOR OUR OWN PEACE AND EMOTIONAL WELLNESS. **FORGIVE!**

- *The young can forgive, they hear the Spirit song much clearer than the adult.*

- *Only the Great Spirit can give you the strength to face the winds and walk the good road.*

- *If you are to succeed you must learn love and understanding.*

- *Build not the illusion of man's falsehoods in your own being!*

FRIENDLINESS

Friendliness is taking an interest in other people.

Friendliness is the important virtue that leads us into many other virtuous behaviors. Friendliness is caring about other people and developing close relations with other people we call friends. It brings about the feeling of welcome and sharing. When you are friendly, you happily share the things you have. You share your time and yourself. Friendliness is going out of your way to make others feel comfortable. Friendliness is sharing the good times and the bad times together. It is caring without being asked to care. Friendliness is the best cure for loneliness. When we are friendly we can do things and share our thoughts and ideas with our friends.

When we make it easy for others to be friends with us we are being friendly. Friendliness means we do not have to be alone unless we want to be. Many people are shy and need a very friendly person to go out of their way before they feel comfortable. Friendliness attracts people and allows them to get to know you and you to know them.

Without friendliness people keep to themselves and have no one to feel close to or to share with. Friendships don't just happen, they are made by people who are willing to be themselves with each other. Without friendliness we would find ourselves alone. Unless we are friendly, people believe we don't like them or care about them.

To be friendly we must sometimes reach out and say "Hello" or "How are you?". Friendliness starts with liking yourself. If you do not feel good about yourself it is difficult to reach out to others. It is not difficult to be friendly no matter where you are. You can nod your head, smile and say "Good day, how are you?". To be a good friend you must show that you care for other people. Having friends is being kind to them and having fun.

IT IS FUN TO BE FRIENDLY. WE SHOULD SMILE AND SAY "HELLO" TO PEOPLE. WE SHOULD SHARE OURSELVES AND SHOW AN INTEREST IN OTHERS. LET US REACH OUT AND BE FRIENDLY WITH ALL PEOPLES.

GENEROSITY

Generosity is a quality of the spirit; it is sharing freely.

Generosity is giving to someone else something that is meaningful to you. It is giving freely without thought about reward, recognition or a gift in return. Giving freely also means you give without concern for what someone does with your gift. It means giving fully, giving a person or group that deserves your help all the help that you can possible give them. It is not giving for praise, or reward. It is seeing an opportunity to share what you have with others and then giving all that you can for the joy of giving. It is one of the best ways to show love.

Without generosity, the world would be a sad place. People who need help would feel like beggars, without pride or dignity. In a world without generosity, every gift would have a string attached. Without generosity people would use gifts to manipulate things for their own advantage. That is not giving. When people give freely, especially when they have had to sacrifice, they are exercising their spirituality. Giving freely and fully is contagious. When one person is generous, it touches other peoples' hearts and then they want to be generous too. This generosity allows more people to receive what they need.

Generosity begins by recognizing the need of other people that deserve your help. We should look for things to share with someone else. We can share our time, our knowledge, even our money. When we give without expecting a return we'll feel good because we have given generously. Give of yourself in a way that makes the recipient feel good. What you have given or shared, let it go. Don't try to control how it is used.

IT MAKES US FEEL GOOD TO BE GENEROUS. WE SHOULD LOOK FOR OPPORTUNITIES TO GIVE AND TO SHARE. LET US ENJOY GIVING FREELY.

Gentleness

Gentleness is acting and speaking in a kind way.

Being gentle means to be very careful. You can be gentle with people and animals in the way you touch them, the way you speak to them. Being gentle with things means to be careful with them so they will not break or be hurt.

Gentleness is using self control in order not to offend anyone. Gentleness is moving wisely, touching softly, holding carefully, speaking quietly and thinking kindly. It is a sign of maturity to develop a gentle disposition, a pure nature and a praiseworthy character. People are very sensitive creatures. Many things are delicate and fragile, but feelings are the most fragile of all. When we are gentle with each other, feelings are protected. When you handle things gently and carefully, it is less likely people will be hurt. We should think gentle thoughts, it makes the world a gentler place. Gentle people are loved and appreciated.

Without gentleness people feelings are hurt often. To be gentle, you have to think about being gentle. We must consciously practice gentleness. No matter how young or old we are, or where we are, we should always practice being gentle. Our voice, our actions, our manners should show a gentleness. After all being a gentlemen or gentlewoman is a very high position; we all can achieve it. It is important when you say something, you say it in a way that does not hurt the listener's feelings. You control yourself so that you don't hurt the other person in any way.

Concentrate your thoughts on love and kindness and people will see the gentleness in your being. Being gentle makes you feel good inside.

> TO BE GENTLE IS TO MATURE. WE MUST THINK, SPEAK AND ACT WITH GENTLENESS. WHEN WE SHOW CARE FOR OTHER PEOPLE WE WILL BE REWARDED BY A CARING RETURN.

Giving

Giving means to grant or bestow on someone else a gift from you.

It is possible that the three greatest virtues are love, justice, and giving. When we are a giving person, it shows that we are not selfish. Once we discover the great purpose of our lives is giving, loving, and serving others in some capacity our world changes to a harmonious, happy one. Many people know that the greatest success you can have in life is unconditional love and giving. Abundance flows when we rise to the loving and giving attitudes that provide for a positive life. A giving person is a happy and joyful being.

It is important to recognize that giving comes in many forms. Giving of your money, your things, material giving is okay. However giving from the heart also consists of giving your time, your kindness, your teaching, your listening, being a friend, supporting another by kind words and deeds. The secret of a joyful happy life is the ability to give. The important thing to know is that giving creates joy in both the giver and receiver.

Giving is a virtue and an attitude that brings the fullness to our lives. When we are stuck in the prison of self and become selfish, we do not give. Selfishness is the opposite of giving. When we become selfish, our world gets smaller, it becomes more difficult. We learn less and begin to experience the negative aspects of life. Once we know that loving and giving empower us and the people around us to have a fulfilled life we become joyous. The act of giving should always be done with a gracious and humble heart with no expectation of return. We should always remember that giving is in alignment with our very purpose in life. <u>Those who cannot give will find it difficult to recognize their purpose.</u>

GIVING IS ESSENTIAL TO OPENING THE DOORS OF A JOYOUS LIFE. GIVING OF LOVE EMPOWERS US TO HIGHER LEVELS OF CAPACITY AND CAPABILITY. WE SHOULD BE DETERMINED THAT OUR SPIRIT BECOMES A LOVING AND GIVING ONE. I WILL FIND AS MANY WAYS TO GIVE THIS DAY AS I CAN. I WILL ENJOY THE PRIVILEGE OF GIVING.

Goodness

Goodness is conforming to virtues, values, and the moral order of the universe.

Goodness is both the practice of excellence and the love of the virtues and how they interact with other people. When we have goodness, we look for the best in all things. We naturally care about other people and how they feel. When we have goodness, we have a favorable character. We should all strive for goodness because goodness is virtuous and just. A person who holds on to the spiritual goodness of our nature has right conduct. We develop good intentions and are kind and benevolent. We find people that have goodness are competent and skillful. They are also loyal and make good friends and associates. The virtue of goodness means we strive for excellence in our character.

Goodness, especially applied to the inner quality of a person, makes them kind, generous, fair, sympathetic, and otherwise generally good. Not only is goodness the inner quality of a person, it also has to do with our behavior and good deeds. This virtue applies to moral excellence, consciously developing particular qualities of life. The good deeds we do for others is also part of our goodness.

A person who has goodness also has principles. They have the discernment to know right from wrong and choose to do the right thing. If everyone would adopt the virtue of goodness, what a wonderful world it would be.

GOODNESS APPLIES TO OUR INNER QUALITIES AND ALSO TO THE GOOD DEEDS WE DO TO HELP OTHERS. I WILL SET AN EXAMPLE OF GOODNESS EACH DAY. I WILL WORK FOR THE HIGH QUALITY OF EXCELLENCE, KINDNESS, AND FRIENDLINESS. I RECOGNIZE THAT THE QUALITY AND VIRTUE OF GOODNESS IS VERY VALUABLE NOT ONLY TO MYSELF BUT TO THE WORLD AROUND ME. I WILL DEVELOP GOODNESS.

GRATITUDE

Gratitude means being deeply grateful or thankful.

Gratitude shows that you appreciate what someone has done for you. It is very important that we learn to appreciate everything we have and what people do for us. It is important that we recognize the help and the gifts from our parents, teachers, and other people we come in contact with. It is important for us to show gratitude to our parents for all the things they provide. When a friend or anyone does a favor for us, we should be grateful and express this thankfulness to them. It is nice to show gratitude by a letter or a card or just kind thankful words.

Much of society today forgets the importance of gratitude. Many individuals take for granted things that are given to them or provided for them. This is not acceptable. Being grateful means we appreciate life itself. We are thankful for everything we have and everything we know. How can we expect to have further gain unless we are thankful and grateful for the things we already have? Being grateful shows the people around us that we are a virtuous person and we do not take things for granted. Even though a mature giver does not expect anything in return, it is still our virtuous duty to express our thankfulness to them. It gives other people pleasure when we say thank you and show our appreciation for all the things that are done for us.

Each day we should be thankful for all the gifts including our life itself. Being grateful and showing appreciation gives satisfaction to all people involved. We should have the attitude of freely giving to the person who has helped us. Gratitude should be shown to others without reason or cause, simply because we are a grateful person. When we show gratitude, it creates a positive response from the other person. No matter how young or old you are, expressing gratitude and thankfulness will be held in high regard.

I WILL BE A GRATEFUL BEING AND EXPRESS THANKFULNESS FOR WHAT I HAVE RECEIVED. I WILL THANK GOD EACH DAY FOR MY LIFE AND ALL OF THE OTHER WONDERFUL THINGS THAT HAVE BEEN GIVEN ME. I WILL APPRECIATE ALL THE THINGS I HAVE, THEREFORE, I WILL SHOW GRATITUDE. A GRATEFUL PERSON IS A VIRTUOUS PERSON.

Helpfulness

Helpfulness is being of service to someone.

Helpfulness is doing something useful for or with other people. When you are being helpful you do things that have a positive effect, that make a difference. Helpfulness can be doing something that a person can not do for themselves, things they don't have time to do, or just things that make life easier for them. Helpfulness is not always doing what other people want. That would be just pleasing people. What people want may not be useful or good for them. We should always try to be helpful to our friends and other people we meet.

You can be helpful to yourself by being sure that you have what you need. We can be helpful to ourselves by eating the right foods, getting enough rest and exercise or wearing proper clothes. You can do things to help your mind and your spirit. One should remember that God is always willing to help if we just ask. Remember helping yourself is OK, you deserve it.

Without helpfulness, everyone would be alone in trying to meet their needs or trying to get things done. If something needs to get done and it takes more than one person, then we need someone to help. Without helpfulness no one would cooperate with each other. We all need help at times. When we practice helpfulness we watch out for each other. You develop an awareness of being helpful by noticing what people need. You look for little opportunities to do a service for them. When you are practicing helpfulness you don't wait for people to ask you. You anticipate what they might need and just do it.

It is very important to learn to help yourself, for if you don't help yourself you will feel helpless. If you don't ask for help you are limiting the possibilities in your life.

WE SHOULD TRY TO BE HELPFUL AND FIND WAYS TO BE OF SERVICE. IT IS VERY IMPORTANT TO OFFER HELP THAT PEOPLE REALLY NEED. BEING HELPFUL IS A MOST HONORABLE VIRTUE.

Honesty

Being honest is being sincere, trustworthy and truthful.

When people are honest, they can be relied upon not to lie, cheat or steal. When honest people tell you something, they really mean it. They would not say something just to get their way or to make an impression. If someone seems nice and friendly, honesty means they really are nice and friendly. They are friendly because they want to be friends, not for hidden reasons. With honesty, you can trust things to be as they appear.

Honesty is telling the truth no matter what. It is being truthful even when admitting the truth could make someone disappointed. Honesty means not exaggerating something just to impress others but telling it like it truly is. Being honest means you don't make false promises. You do what you said you would do. Your actions match your words. The most important part of honesty is integrity in doing what we'll say we'll do.

People are supposed to learn to trust. Without honesty, people would always have to be suspicious. Without honesty, people could lie, cheat or steal. Sometimes people aren't honest with themselves. They try to pretend that something doesn't matter, even when it really does, like hurting someone's feelings. When someone isn't honest with themselves, they usually are not honest with others. Honesty keeps you from deceiving or fooling other people just to get what you want. Honesty also helps you to not fool yourself. Use your imagination but don't let it keep you from telling the truth. When you are honest with yourself you have a chance to correct your mistakes. When you are honest with others, they know they can believe you. Be honest with yourself and you will always be able to be honest with others.

WE SHOULD BUILD OUR WORLD WITH HONESTY AND INTEGRITY. WE SHOULD TELL THE TRUTH AND RESPECT OTHERS' PROPERTY. IT IS IMPORTANT TO USE KINDNESS, TACT OR SILENCE RATHER THAN HURTING SOMEONE JUST TO BE HONEST.

Honorableness

To be honorable is living by the virtues.

Being honorable is to live with honor, with a sense of respect for what you believe to be right. It is in essence living by these virtues, living up to the gifts that God placed within you. When you are honorable, you are worthy of the respect of others. You set a good example. When we are honorable we follow the wise, the intelligent, the learned, the enduring, the dutiful, the noble; one should follow a good and wise pattern.

When you are being honorable, you don't feel ashamed of who you are or what you are doing. You feel proud of the choices you are making. Other people admire a person who is honorable and they want to be honorable themselves.

Without honor, people act disrespectfully and do things which make them and others feel bad. People without honor don't care about the virtues, they do just what they want without thinking if it is right or wrong. When someone practices being honorable, other people know they can be trusted to do their best and try their hardest. Their word of honor means something.

When you want to be honorable, it helps to realize that you were created noble, capable of practicing all the virtues. Staying noble is up to you. When you are being honorable, you respect your special gifts. You respect yourself. You make efforts to practice all the virtues you know because they are the building blocks of a noble person.

In the pursuit of honor we must never give up on ourselves. We should recognize the importance of keeping agreements that treat others with respect. The practice of virtues should be a daily endeavor so that we can recognize that we are a worthy and noble person. You should strive constantly to develop an honorable condition for yourself.

Humility

Humility is to be humble.

Humility and humbleness allow us to realize that we are no more important than any one else. They produce an attitude that allows us to learn from our mistakes. It means doing your best without attracting undue attention to yourself. It means to pay attention to what you have yet to learn rather than what you have already done. Humility is serving for the love of self and our human brothers and sisters - not to impress them. Humility is important because it keeps you focused on your own growth rather than the faults of others. If you worry about impressing others, they will start to tell you what they want you to be and you will lose a part of your own identity. Humility helps you learn from mistakes rather than being ashamed of them. Humility helps you treat others as equals, different yet equal. Humility lets you learn from everyone around you. It keeps you free from prejudice and from judging others.

When you are a confident, humble person you do not pay a lot of attention to what others say about you, good or bad. Don't spend your energy trying to impress others. All people with class show humbleness and humility. Just be yourself and do your best. It is very important to acknowledge what you accomplish; however, these accomplishments do not make you better than others.

Being humble is a very empowering virtue. It allows you to see reality and to have a more harmonious life. Humbleness has been a virtue of almost all of the great kind leaders of history. Humbleness allows you to see and hear of the great things of life. More respect is given to the humble person than to the arrogant one.

I WILL ALWAYS ENDEAVOR TO BE HUMBLE. I WILL LEARN FROM MY MISTAKES. I WILL NOT JUDGE OTHERS OR MYSELF. I VALUE MY ABILITY TO KEEP GROWING AND RECOGNIZING THE TRUTH OF MY LIFE THROUGH BEING HUMBLE.

IDEALISM

Idealism means believing in making the world a better place.

When we have high ideas we really care about what is right and meaningful in life. When you are an idealist you don't just accept things the way they are. You believe they are supposed to be and should be better. In being an idealist you see the world as a better place than presently exists. You believe it so much that you are willing to work very hard to make it happen. You don't ignore problems when you see them, like people going hungry or someone being treated unjustly. To be an idealist is to recognize that we have a dysfunctional school system, families, divorced and separated and in disharmony, and the workplace a battle ground void of the understanding of harmony, efficiency and caring; you want to make a difference.

Idealist dare to have big dreams and then act as if they are possible. They can imagine something better, define it and then do it. Idealism does not mean that you are an idle dreamer. For idle dreamers just wish that things were better. Idealists plan and do something to make things better. When people don't have ideas, they just live as if nothing matters very much. They have no imagination or dreams of what is possible. They usually just settle for whatever happens. People without ideas don't strive to improve the conditions of our world. It is our innate job to be somewhat idealistic. If there were no idealism, then things would just stay as they are. No one would have a vision of how things could be better or even what is possible. The best they could hope for is that things wouldn't get worse. Without idealistic hope, people would get more and more discouraged.

When you recognize the importance of having ideas you know that tomorrow will be better than today. You know what is possible and you can help to make it happen. When you develop idealism the first step is to visualize wonderful possibilities. You look at where you are and where the world around you is and where you want to go and how you can help your fellow man and you make a plan to get there. People that accomplish great things have all started with an idea, a dream. We must be very careful that we do not allow other people to interfere with our dream or our idea. When you make your plan you must stick to it no matter what. There are two very important aspects of being an idealist. One is to ask God to guide you always and the second is in practicing the virtues which is a great way to make the ideal real in your life. Virtuous Idealism can change the world for the better!

> I WILL DEVELOP IDEAS, THOUGHTS, HOPES AND DREAMS. I WILL HAVE FAITH THAT WITH GOD'S HELP I CAN MAKE A DIFFERENCE THROUGH MY DEVELOPING HIGH IDEALS. I WILL BEHAVE AND DEVELOP THE ATTITUDE THAT MY IDEAS ARE ALREADY REALITY.

- *Go beyond your present status; it is time to expand your knowledge.*

- *These virtues are the foundations of goodness.*

- *Keep your bio-computer free from junk and virus.*

- *Learn that the process of positive thought brings positive results.*

INTEGRITY

Integrity means the quality of being honorable and upright in character and actions.

Integrity is shown by your character of having very high standards of right and wrong. Integrity means you are whole, that you understand virtues and the proper way to behave and treat others in all situations. When we have integrity, we can be trusted and people recognize and respect us for our integrity. When we strive to develop integrity, we become a complete person. Spiritual, intellectual, and physical health is a gift that comes with the wholeness of integrity.

When we approach a project or a lesson with integrity, we will be able to complete the project because determination is part of integrity. The effort of integrity gives us the things we need to complete projects with excellence. Each one of us must recognize the importance of integrity for good, healthy growth of wisdom and knowledge. Integrity is the combination of many virtues in action that become part of our character. Each one of us should strive daily to become more aware of building character with integrity. We must remember that integrity builds a wholeness and an excellent condition in all things.

Without integrity, people could not trust each other. It would be a world of incompleteness. A great part of our society today lacks the understanding of virtues, values, principles, and morality and, therefore, lacks integrity. Without integrity, the individual and society at large can become dysfunctional for they no longer are held together with the fibers of integrity. Integrity and honesty are forever connected. Our character should always excel in both.

I WILL APPLY INTEGRITY TO EVERYTHING I DO. IT WILL BECOME ONE OF THE MOST IMPORTANT ASPECTS OF MY CHARACTER. I WILL HAVE INTEGRITY AND ALWAYS REACH FOR VERY HIGH STANDARDS. I WILL BE A PERSON OF INTEGRITY.

JOYFULNESS

Joyfulness is being filled up inside with happiness, peace, love and a sense of well being.

Joyfulness is the inward feeling of peace and the outward behavior of spiritual joy. Joy is in all of us. It comes from a sense of purpose and love. Joy comes from an appreciation for the gift of life. It comes when we are doing what we know is right. Joy is related to fun, but is not exactly the same. Fun comes from what is happening outside, having a good time. Joy comes from what is happening inside.

Joyfulness is always there regardless of what is happening on the outside. You can use this inner joy in anything you do. When we are joyful, any job, any chore, anything we have to do we know we can do with joyfulness. No matter what life brings us, we can look inside and find our joy and make our work a joyful job.

Joy is the inner sense that can carry us through hard times, even when we are feeling very sad. It is very important to know that without inner joy, a spiritual condition, all of our feelings are determined by what is happening to us. When things are going well on the outside, we feel good. When things are going wrong on the outside, we feel bad. Without the inner sense of joy we feel bounced around by the pain and the pleasure of others and whatever is happening to us. If we are joyful, things still happen to us, but we handle them with a spiritual strength.

Remember, joyfulness comes from your spirit, you find it inside yourself! When you look inside yourself you will know that God created you and you are loved! Remember that life is His gift to you. Remember that you are God's gift to the world. You are a noble and joyful being. Let yourself feel your inner peace and joy even when things are tough.

WE SHOULD BE THANKFUL FOR THE JOY WE FEEL INSIDE. WE MUST JOYFULLY GO THROUGH LIFE IN OUR WORK AND OUR PLAN. ONE OF THE MOST IMPORTANT VIRTUES OF LIFE IS TO RECOGNIZE YOUR SPIRITUAL INNER POWER AND BECOME A JOYFUL PERSON.

JUSTICE

Justice means people receive fairness for what they deserve.

Justice demands a caring and discerning attitude by individuals, organizations and society at large. Each person should know justice and practice it. Justice has two sides. The side of punishment and that of reward. As we go through life, we should constantly develop a caring attitude for your own rights and the rights of others. If someone is taking advantage of you, it is not just to allow them to continue doing it. If someone is hurting you, it is just to stop them. Justice means that every persons rights are protected. When you practice being just, you treat each person as an individual. You don't judge people or put them in categories, you just see them one by one.

Without justice, the world can be a cruel and dangerous place where prejudice of race, sex or religion actually develops injustice. These unjust prejudices develop the most negative aspect of humanity: hatred. When justice is practiced, people can expect to receive what they deserve. When we do something well and there is justice, we will be rewarded for it. If we are accused of something when justice prevails, we will have a chance to be heard fairly. When there is justice, everyone receives fairness. When we practice justice we must investigate truth for ourselves, accepting what others say is only their opinion. We must investigate the facts with our own minds. We must learn to think for ourselves.

When you are just, you admit your own mistakes and accept the consequences. When you practice justice you don't gossip or find fault behind someone's back. It wouldn't be fair because they are not there to tell their side of things. If you have a problem with someone, you go directly to that person and work things out. When you are being just, you stand up for yourself and for others.

BEING A CHAMPION FOR JUSTICE TAKES COURAGE. SOMETIMES WHEN YOU STAND FOR JUSTICE IT MAY SEEM LIKE YOU STAND ALONE, BUT IN FACT, YOU ARE A CHAMPION FOR JUSTICE.

KINDNESS

Kindness is being concerned about the welfare of others.

Kindness is a most important virtue for it opens your character to practice many other positive virtues. Kindness is showing you care about anyone or anything that crosses your path. You can be kind to people, to animals and to the environment. Kindness means to care for others and the earth as much or more than you care about yourself. Kindness makes for a happy meeting or renewal of a friendship. It is the condition that can develop a harmonious and caring environment.

A kind person is gracious and giving. Kindness is sometimes shown in small gestures that brighten other people's lives. Kindness towards all created things and beings is essential for happiness. Kindness is especially showing love to someone who is sad or needs your help. Without kindness no one would listen when people or animals need help. Without kindness everyone would be more selfish and they would be just looking out for themselves. The world would be very lonely without kindness. When you reach out to another in an act of kindness everyone benefits. Everything in the world is inter-connected. If we are unkind to any part of it, it affects us all.

When you are kind, you become sensitive to the world around you. You notice when someone or something needs your care. Your being kind is not for a selected few, kindness must become a consistent virtue within your being.

REMEMBER, BEING KIND MAKES THINGS BETTER FOR EVERY ONE OF US. WHEN YOU ARE TEMPTED TO BE CRUEL, TO CRITICIZE, OR EVEN TEASE, A KIND PERSON IMMEDIATELY DECIDES NOT TO DO IT. IT IS YOUR OBLIGATION TO FIND KINDER WAYS TO DO ALL THINGS. KINDNESS IS ITS OWN REWARD!

LOVE

Love is a special feeling that makes you want to do nice things for people.

To love each other is a command of God. Thou shall love thy neighbor as thyself. Do unto others as you would have them do unto you. There are many reasons to believe that when one matures they become a loving person. **The supreme happiness of life is the conviction that we are loved. To be loved - LOVE!** Unconditional love brings human kind to a very high level of maturity. A loving person cares about people, they want to be near them and want to share with them. Loving means treating people with special care and kindness because they have the same needs and desires as you do.

A loving person treats other people just like you would like them to treat you, with care and respect. Being loving is putting yourself in someone else's shoes and accepting them just as they are. You can even be loving to strangers. You should love yourself and you must above all love the Creator.

Without love the world can be a lonely place. When people feel they are not loved, they become unhappy. Sometimes, they will act angry and treat others carelessly. They don't let others get close to them and they have trouble sharing and trusting. Love is a binding emotion and virtue that brings us all closer together.

Everyone likes to be loved. When you are being a loving person, you help others to feel important. When people know when they are loved, they are nicer and kinder. Love is contagious. It keeps spreading. When you love God, you will be able to feel His love for you. When you love yourself, you have more love to give.

It is important to know that love and justice are two extremely important virtues. They bring about the empowerment of peace and harmony, human rights and freedom.

You must allow yourself to feel love. Sometimes it just comes naturally. Showing that you care is a way to be loving. You can do all kinds of thoughtful little things to show love. You can share your time and yourself. your ideas, your feelings, your opinions, your affection.

Being loving is showing compassion for other people and wishing for them what you wish for yourself. A loving person is not prejudiced, does not pre-judge other people. We must nurture the virtue of love for it is the empowerment of all good things.

I WILL BE A LOVING AND JOYOUS PERSON. I WILL SHOW MY LOVE WITH THOUGHTFUL ACTS, KIND WORDS AND AFFECTION. I WILL TREAT OTHERS AS I WANT TO BE TREATED. I WILL LOVE GOD AND ALL THAT HE CREATED, INCLUDING MYSELF.

- *Get ready for your immortality, love this life and live it bravely.*

- *You can do it.*

- *Be not a faultfinder - everything has two sides, or more.*

- *God has a purpose for every life.*

Loyalty

Loyalty is standing up for something you believe in with unwavering faith.

Loyalty is being faithful to family, country, friends or ideals. It is standing by a person when the going gets tough as well as when things are good. When you are a loyal friend, even if someone disappoints or hurts you, you still hang in there with them. When you are loyal you don't change from day to day. You stay true to someone or something unless you have a reason to believe that your loyalty has been betrayed.

Loyalty is based on commitments that you make and plan to keep forever. When you are loyal, people know what you stand for. Your friends and family know that you will support them no matter what happens. When you are loyal to your commitment people know that nothing can come between you.

Loyalty seems to be a virtue that is not practiced a lot today. When we are a loyal person we build friendships that last forever. A person who does not have loyalties can't be counted on when the going gets tough, they go away. Those that counted on them for support are betrayed. People who are worthy of your loyalty can trust that they will never have to stand alone.

You can develop loyalty by making a commitment to a person, country, or ideal. You should be very careful about choosing what you commit yourself to because if you are loyal, you will stand behind that commitment for a long time. Loyalty is being strong in what you believe or care about. It is safeguarding something or someone you believe in. When you are loyal you are worthy of trust.

I WILL BE LOYAL TO THE PEOPLE I CARE ABOUT. I WILL BE A GOOD FRIEND THROUGH GOOD TIMES AND BAD. I WILL BE LOYAL TO WHAT I KNOW IS RIGHT.

MERCY

Merciful means to treat others with compassion and forgiveness.

Justice is giving people what they deserve. Mercy is giving people more than they deserve. Mercy is a quality of the heart. When you are merciful you are willing to forgive even when you have been hurt.

Being merciful is being willing to start over, to wipe the slate clean of all mistakes or hurts and give people another chance. God is very merciful to us - by giving us lots of blessings and a lot of chances to keep learning from our mistakes. Mercy means you feel for someone who is suffering and do something to help them. A mercy is a blessing. When we are merciful we give others the gift of tenderness.

Mercy takes the harshness and cruelty out of our world. Without mercy it would be a dark and miserable place. Being merciful gives us the opportunity to help other people to heal their hurts. We forgive each other and the relationships between us heal. Being kind when someone has made a mistake, when someone is in need, is a good way of being merciful. It is forgiving others, it is showing compassion and tenderness for people who are suffering. You can help people and be merciful even if you don't know them. We must be careful that being merciful, when someone really needs an act of justice in order to learn, doesn't really help them.

> I WILL SHOW MERCY TO OTHERS. I WILL PUT MYSELF IN THEIR SHOES AND DO WHAT I CAN TO BE HELPFUL. I WILL NOT IGNORE THEM. I WILL GIVE OTHERS ANOTHER CHANCE IF THEY MAKE A MISTAKE. I WILL LISTEN TO MY HEART.

MODERATION

Moderation is having enough, not too much or not too little.

Moderation means we do not become extravagant. It means you don't do the same thing all the time. You create balance in your life. Becoming a workaholic or working all the time, or playing all the time is not being moderate. Being moderate is studying enough and playing enough and working enough. Moderation is stopping before you go overboard in anything you do.

Too little of something is as bad as too much of something. People who talk too much can be disruptive. People who don't talk much at all, get ignored and when there is a discussion, their special way of thinking about things is missing.

Moderation is the virtue that keeps us from being blown about in the reckless winds of our desires. When we do not live in moderation, we tend to live in extremes. When we live in extremes we tend to waste a lot of our life. When we have moderation we grow healthy in body, mind and spirit. Without moderation people can get swept away and damage themselves with things like drugs and alcohol.

Without moderation, people get too greedy. Without moderation, people don't do enough.

Moderation establishes balance. It is important to keep the balance so that we do our share of the work and participate in a moderate degree in play. Without moderation we can start getting addicted to things and want more and more. Even things you like can hurt you if you have too much - like too much television. When people have too much of something, they can find themselves out of control.

Moderation keeps us from being controlled by our desires. When we develop moderation as a virtue, we create a sense of balance in our lives. With moderation, we are much more likely to get what we actually need. When we strive for balanced moderation, we benefit and other people do too.

Learning proper limits is the first step in moderation. Moderation produces wisdom and self control. Wisdom is the fact of being sure that you get what you need. Self control is stopping yourself before things go too far.

One of the most important aspects of moderation is the prediction of any addiction. Addictions of any kind are not good for us. It could be TV or computer games, or food or addiction to another person or to any of the drugs that we know we should not get involved with. When you are working hard for balanced moderation, you can trust yourself and others can too.

> I WILL STRIVE FOR BALANCED MODERATION. I WILL BE THANKFUL AND CONTENT TO GET WHAT I NEED. I WILL WORK OUT A BALANCED PROGRAM OF WORK AND PLAY IN MY LIFE. MODERATION WILL KEEP ME FROM ANY ADDICTION.

- *Share thoughts and words of comfort.*

- *See sameness, honor diversity.*

- *Insight becomes clearer as we learn to love.*

- *Your soul always maintains its dignity: so should you!*

Modesty

Modesty is having a sense of quiet self respect.

Modesty is to value yourself to have a sense of privacy about your being. Modesty can be expressed in a number of ways. It comes when you have a sense of self acceptance and quiet pride. Modesty means having a sense of what is appropriate and inappropriate about showing yourself, your body, as well as how you allow others to touch you. Modesty also means to accept praise without getting conceited with a feeling of superiority. You are grateful for your blessings and your gifts.

Modesty and humbleness are similar. A modest person does not brag or boast. Without modesty, people tend to brag and their virtues get lost in the noise. Bragging puts other people off, so immodest people can become quite lonely. When we are modest, we don't need to tell others how great we are. We can be known by our actions in our work and let our virtues speak for us. People who are modest show self respect and then others respect them too.

Modesty is an attitude. It begins by being comfortable with yourself. It is knowing that you have special gifts and that others do as well.

Humility helps in the development of modesty. When you are being modest you are comfortable being yourself. You respect yourself. You set boundaries about your rights. It is important in the endeavor of life to share the credit with others who deserve it. A modest person lets their actions speak louder than their words.

I will develop modesty. I have no need to brag because I have confidence within my own self. I am worthy of healthy attention just as I am.

OBEDIENCE

Obedience is living by the rules and laws which people in authority have made to guide and protect us.

Obedience is listening to authority and obeying the rules. Obedience is listening to what your parents and others have to say and following it as faithfully as you can. Obedience should be given to your parents, your teachers, the laws of the country in which you live and to God. Obedience to God means you abide by the spiritual laws of your religion, such as the Ten Commandments. The first commandment is to honor your father and your mother. Obedience to God is very connected to how well you obey your parents and other certain authority figures.

Obedience is following the rules even when no one is watching what you do. Being obedient keeps us safe and happy. If people didn't care about obeying rules, they would do just what they wanted, even when it hurt themselves and other people. There are many dangers in the world. The laws and rules are put in society to protect us. If parents didn't give their guidance, the world would not be very safe for you. Although it is sometimes difficult to follow and be obedient to the rules, we must trust those who are in authority by obeying their laws and rules created to protect us.

When we obey spiritual laws, like the Golden Rule, your spirit grows strong and you have a happier life.

Obedience begins by realizing that those in authority know what is best and care about you. We must make a special effort to learn the rules at home, in the work place or in school. We should also learn about the laws of our religion. Obedience is taking responsibility for following the rules. Obedience is about trusting in God, your parents, elders and teachers. Be respectful of those in authority when they tell you what to do, even if you don't agree with it or understand it. If you need to question a rule or decision, do it respectfully and abide by the final decision.

One of the most important aspects of obedience is that if you break a rule, and suffer a consequence or punishment, have the courage to learn from your mistake.

I WILL BE AN OBEDIENCE PERSON. I WILL LISTEN RESPECTFULLY TO MY ELDERS AND DO WHAT I AM SUPPOSED TO DO IN OBEYING LAWS AND RULES. I WILL OBEY THE LAWS OF MY COUNTRY. IT IS INCUMBENT ON EVERY MATURING PERSON TO OBEY THE VIRTUES FOR THEY ARE THE UNIVERSAL LAW FOR THE BETTERMENT OF ALL PEOPLES.

- *In stillness and quiet we find great things!*

- *In stillness commune with your soul, it is waiting to hear from you.*

- *In stillness and quiet we find great things!*

- *In stillness commune with your soul, it is waiting to hear from you.*

Orderly

Orderly means being neat and organized.

Being orderly is important in all aspects of life, from family, to school, to the workplace. It gives us as individuals a sense of harmony. An orderly person keeps things you use in a particular place so that when you need them you can immediately find them. Being orderly means being organized so that we are ready to go at a moments notice. An orderly person plans their work and their play. When we do things in an orderly fashion we do them step by step instead of going in circles and wasting time. Being orderly makes it easier to accomplish any task. An orderly person is also well behaved, obeying the rules of family, school or workplace.

An orderly person creates a neat environment that is harmonious. It allows us to achieve excellence easier. Of course an orderly person keeps their room neat and clean and assists other members of the family in taking care of their home.

When there is an order about your life you can recognize a problem or mistake and correct it easier. There is an order that is proper in everything in the universe. When you learn to appreciate the order of creation, you will see the beauty and harmony of all living things. When you are not an orderly person you are not in tune with these natural harmonies and they can cause you the feeling of being lost and confused. People who need to do things precisely and quickly need to be especially orderly. When people don't behave in an orderly way or within the rules, it creates confusion and unhappiness. Things get all mixed up when people are not orderly. When you are orderly you can take any problem and plan a solution. If you have made a big mistake, you can put it right. You can in fact create order around you. It makes your soul feel peaceful.

It is important to notice how you feel in your particular environment. The environment, no matter where it is or what it is, should be clean and orderly for it will bring harmony to that place. You should create an harmonious space that makes your soul peaceful and also brings peace to those around you.

I WILL LIVE EACH DAY WITH ORDER, PUTTING THINGS AWAY NEATLY AND PLANNING THE JOBS I HAVE TO DO. I WILL CREATE BEAUTY AND HARMONY IN MY SPACE AND IN MY LIFE BY BEING ORDERLY.

PATIENCE

Patience is being calm and tolerant.

Patience is quiet hope and expectation based on trust that, in the end, everything will be all right. Patience means waiting. It is enduring a delay or troublesome situation without complaining. It means having self control because you can't control the way someone else is acting or when things don't go as you like.

Patience is persevering, sticking with something for as long as it takes to finish it. When you are patience, you know that things take time. Patience is also a commitment to the future. It is doing something now so that later something good will happen. It is also putting up with all of the things necessary to make it happen. Patience is seeing the end in the beginning, doing what you can and then calmly waiting, with trust that the results will come.

Today people seem to have trouble being patient. Without patience people want everything now. They have trouble doing things now which will have a good result later. Without patience, people can't stand to wait for anyone and fuss the whole time, which makes them and everyone else upset. When people are impatient they become irritable when things don't go their way or people around them make mistakes.

It is important in helping yourself and people around you to be both kind and patient. When people make mistakes, if we are impatient with them, it makes them more tense and things just get worse.

Although each day in life is important, it is also wise to be patient and plan things that will pay off in the future. When we are patient we have less of a chance of becoming discouraged. We trust that our goals are worth the wait and the work for future accomplishment.

A patience person is not a complainer or a critic of everything. They forgive other people and themselves. A patient person makes the world a kinder and gentler place, and other people feel safe around them. A patient person usually has a sense of humor, because it helps! When you are a patient person you kindly hold to something that you have to endure. You are gentle with others and you are gentle with yourself. With patience you persevere and endure, even when things get difficult or tiresome.

Trust in God can give you patience, a quiet hope that will get you through hard times.

I WILL BECOME A PATIENT PERSON. I WILL BE GENTLE WITH OTHERS AND MYSELF WHEN WE MAKE MISTAKES. I WILL SET GOALS AND PERSEVERE UNTIL MY GOALS ARE WON. I WILL TRUST IN GOD THAT ALL WILL TURN OUT WELL.

- *Love opens ourselves to an intensity of consciousness we did not know was possible before.*

- *The true Spirit has established the ignorant upon the seats of learning.*

- *Be not lost in the wilds of remoteness and nothingness where prejudice and hatred abide.*

- *If you will look, the universe is pregnant with manifold bounties awaiting your spiritual acceptance.*

Peacefulness

Peacefulness is to feel peaceful.

Peace and peacefulness is the present call of the world. Blessed are the peace makers. Today both peace between all peoples and peacefulness within ourselves is of the utmost desire and importance.

Peacefulness in the individual is an inner sense of calm. It comes from a person who respects others and the environments. It is a way of getting quiet and looking at things so that you can understand them. It is facing your fears and then letting them go. A peaceful person is a trusting person, for they know their life will be all right.

Peacefulness is giving up the love of power for the power of love. It is practicing justice, which means to be fair to yourself and others. Peacefulness is a way of approaching conflict with others so no one is made wrong. Everyone wins, because you work to find a peaceful solution. Peace comes when you give up violence, prejudice and thinking of others as enemies. Peacefulness comes from an awareness that all human beings are part of one human family. Peace in the world begins with peace in your heart and peace in your interactions with others.

In order to be a peaceful being, one should spend quiet time thinking and meditating. A peaceful heart is one which is free of trouble or worry. It allows you to trust. It is a quieting of your spirit, a willingness to enter your own inner stillness. Without peacefulness, you feel like you have to control everyone and everything.

World peace is not only something that governments can create, while all the rest of us sit there waiting for them to do it. People make peace in their homes and schools and work places. The process of world peace in the future will not only be about governments, it will be about the unification of all the peoples in the world and the recognition that their differences are exciting and interesting.

Peacefulness absolutely allows us to remain free of violence, free from prejudice, safe from injustice. When each of us is peaceful, all those who come in contact with us are loved, respected and judged fairly. Differences are seen as benefits rather than reasons to fight. The peace in our lives leads to peace in the world.

Today we must all work diligently toward peacefulness, for without peacefulness, differences become a threat, people tend to judge others by hearsay. Without peace, no one is safe. Without peace, we have violence, injustice, prejudice or inequality. There is always fear and resentment. This can happen in a family, or between nations. It leads to fights and wars. And no one ever really wins a war. When you are a person striving for peacefulness you will become a peacemaker, you will use peaceful language, you will be kind and assisting to others. When you are a peacemaker, there is no violence in your life. The chances of you being harmed are greatly reduced. There is always a win-win situation available when you practice being a peacemaker.

AS A LOVER OR PEACE AND PEACEFULNESS, I WILL SEE OTHERS WITH MY OWN EYES AND NOT THROUGH THE EYES OF OTHERS. I WILL SEEK PEACE BY USING PEACEFUL LANGUAGE AND FINDING PEACEFUL SOLUTIONS FOR ANY PROBLEM THAT ARISES. I WILL FIND MY INNER PEACE AND LET IT CARRY ME GENTLY EACH DAY.

- *Whatever the blessed colors of man; if we are cut we all bleed red. Our hurt is pain, our healing the same.*

- *It is essential for your wellness to love everyone. "Love your enemies, do good to them that hate you."*

- *Witness the mysteries of your own resurrection, see its truth.*

- *Do not be among the invalid souls who have confined the lands of knowledge within the walls of self and passion.*

PRAYERFULNESS

Prayer is talking with God.

Prayerfulness is absolutely important for the betterment for every individual and the world at large. The answers to individual and global problems can be found in the communication with almighty God. Prayerfulness can be practiced in many ways. You can pray in silence or out loud. You can sing or dance your prayer. You can use any language. God always hears your thoughts and understands your heart.

Prayerfulness is living in a way which shows that you are in the presence of your creator. It is doing simple things with an attitude of being grateful. It is knowing you are a unique creation of God, and acting in ways which are worthy of that gift of life. Prayer is praising God, being thankful for things. Praying is quiet reflection. It is allowing the great spirit to speak to you. It is listening and receiving God's guidance. One must be careful in prayer not to just talk. We certainly can not get the answers without being still and not listening. Some say praying is talking to God and meditation is listening.

You can pray to God at any time. Prayerfulness is sharing your hopes and your problems, the things you feel ashamed of and the things you feel proud of. A praying person has actually come into the presence of God with their wishes, desires and gratefulness. We must believe and trust that god fully understands our worries, thoughts, hopes and dreams, for this is faith.

Prayer makes things clear when we are confused, gives us hope when we feel sad, gives us answers when we have problems, and provides strength to face the challenges of life. When we are a prayerful person and need answers, we must become very still and turn to God. Let God know all that is in your heart, as if you were talking to your very best friend. Trust His wisdom and don't expect that everything you ask will happen, for many things we perceive to be good for us are not, He knows best! Listen and notice what happens.

Prayer can be answered in many ways. A thought or idea may come to you while you are reflecting. You might have a dream that gives you an answer. The holy spirit may speak to you through the actions or the words of another person. You may start to see things differently. When you pray, be ready to receive an answer. The feeling of love must pervade every prayer. The feeling of love and connection in prayer and meditation should not stop when you finish praying. Prayer and communion with God is actually a continuum. It is part of life that you do, consciously and subconsciously, when you are a mature prayerful person.

THANK YOU GOD FOR THE GIFT OF PRAYER. IT IS IMPORTANT THAT I SEEK THE TRUTH WITH ALL MY HEART AND ALL MY BEING AND THE TRUTH WILL SET ME FREE. I CAN FIND THIS TRUTH BY CONSTANT PRAYER.

- *Do not seek love; be love.*

- *Be in love with God first. All good things will come.*

- *Kindle the fire of love and burn away all bad things.*

- *Set your foot onto the Lord of agape love, then harmony and peace will come.*

Purpose

Purposeful means acting on purpose with a plan.

Every human being has a purpose, a primary purpose, a secondary purpose and many smaller purposes. Being purposeful is having a good reason for doing something and sticking with it.

A purposeful person has a clear focus instead of being fuzzy or unsure of what they are doing or why they are doing it. When you have a goal you are working toward, you are being purposeful. To be purposeful means to concentrate on something. Concentrate your mind and your efforts so that something good will happen as a result of your determined purpose. You must stay faithful to your purpose no matter what.

It is important that we each seek and find our primary purpose in life. This could mean the job or profession in which we will spend most of our life making a living. Today we must be sure that it is a job or a profession that fulfills us monetarily and spiritually. Our secondary purpose could be what hobbies do we choose. How do we spend our leisure time with our family and friends.

It is not a purposeful way to just let things happen. A purposeful person makes things happen properly. A dedicated, purposeful person can achieve just about anything.

A person who is not purposeful can lose their own identity and become confused. They will lose track of what they are doing, let themselves be distracted, and their efforts will be lost. Without a sense of purpose, people wouldn't know the reasons why they are doing something, so when the going gets tough, they tend to give up. Without a clear purpose, we would probably become scattered. Without concentrated efforts, nothing gets accomplished. Without purpose people tend to do a little of this and a little of that, and never really finish anything. Without purpose much of our life can be wasted. We all must recognize that we were intended to be persons of purpose.

You must choose to be purposeful, so you can accomplish great things. You will have a vision or goal for what you want to do. You will act in a concentrated and focused way. You will see the results of your efforts. A purposeful person is always motivated because they know why they are doing something.

Being purposeful begins when you decide to do something that matters to you or someone important to you. A purposeful person decides to build or create something that is important even if it is difficult.

> I WILL FIND, STUDY AND RECOGNIZE MY INTENDED PURPOSE. I WILL BE CLEAR ABOUT WHAT I AM DOING AND WHY. I WILL DEVELOP CONCENTRATED PURPOSE IN MY LIFE. WITH GOD'S HELP, I CAN ACCOMPLISH GREAT THINGS.

Reliability

Reliability means others can depend on you.

Reliability is doing something you agreed to do in a predictable way, without forgetting or having to be reminded. When you are a reliable person, other people know they can count on you to do the things you have agreed to do and do them on time. If something outside of your control happens, and you are kept from doing what you have promised, it isn't your fault. However, we should notify these people who are relying on us as soon as possible. People know that you really care about them when you are reliable. Other people can relax, knowing the task is in your reliable hands.

If we couldn't rely on each other, we would have to do everything ourselves. Unless people are reliable, we can't count on them. If a person does what they are supposed to do sometimes and other times not, we can't be sure they will do it at an important time. In every endeavor of life, from business to games, it is important that every player on the team is reliable. The family unit itself demands reliability on the part of all its' members. If a friend or someone in your family is not reliable, we can never know for sure if they will do what they promised. If we are not reliable it creates anxiety and distrust.

If our nation's transportation was not reliable, passengers would miss important appointments. When you are reliable, you treat every job as a sacred trust and dedicate yourself to being reliable. Reliability gives us a sense of safety and peace.

It is important to dedicate yourself to being reliable, taking responsibility seriously, like a sacred trust. When you are reliable you make sure that what you have promised gets done, unless it was impossible. Those who make proper plans and serve others by being reliable will create a sense of well being within themselves.

I WILL BE RELIABLE. I WILL KEEP MY COMMITMENTS WITHOUT BEING REMINDED. OTHERS WILL BE ABLE TO COUNT ON ME. NOTHING WILL STOP ME FROM GIVING MY VERY BEST.

RESPECT

Respect means to honor other people and their rights.

It is more important esteeming others more highly than ourselves - this shows high respect. Being respectful is reflected in the courtesy with which we treat one another. Respectfulness is also very important in how we treat other peoples' belongings and property. Speaking and acting respectfully gives people the dignity they deserve. We should treat everyone we meet with respect until they prove differently. It is particularly important to be respectful of elderly people, of your elders, like your parents, grandparents and teachers. Because they have lived longer they have accumulated more wisdom and can teach you many things if you show them respect and kindness.

Our elders deserve a special measure of courtesy and respect, for they have contributed much to your life and to society. Although you have a right to your opinion, it is more important to listen to them and to honor their ways. A respectful society is more peaceful and orderly.

Being respectful includes self-respect. You should respect your own rights and protect them. Every woman, man and child is a creation of God and all deserve respect. Without respectfulness, people's privacy would be violated. Anyone who felt like it would read private letters or walk into places where other people wanted privacy. Without respect people speak rudely to each other and treat others as if they don't matter. Without self-respect you would let others hurt you or use you. Respectfulness makes people feel valued. Without respect for laws or rules, we would just have chaos. When you respect other people's property, they are more likely to respect yours. When you treat your self with respect, others respect you too.

When one is being respectful, they think how they would like to be treated and then treat others that same way. Respectfulness creates a nice condition concerning your belongings and property and your right to privacy. We all ought to be respected and have dignity. We must all learn to treat other people's space and their environment with respect.

Being respectful is speaking quietly and being courteous to all people, especially to our elders. We should practice using the kind words: "excuse me", "please" and "thank you". When learning to be respectful, one must always keep in mind that there is always more than one way to see and express things.

> I WILL TREAT EVERYONE WITH RESPECT. I WILL SHOW COURTESY AND OBEDIENCE TO MY ELDERS AND LEARN FROM THEIR WISDOM. I WILL RESPECT OTHER PEOPLES' RIGHTS, THEIR BELONGINGS AND THEIR PROPERTY. I WILL SHOW RESPECT.

- *Be sharp of eye, your sight will gaze on truth and wisdom.*

- *Every person stands on their own personal responsibility.*

- *Going against God's wishes and rules causes misery. Your best bet is obedience.*

- *Men create taboos for themselves, out of superstition for selfish ends enforce them in the name of religion. Nothing is more reprehensible.*

Responsibility

Responsibility means being responsible for others and self.

Acting responsibly is a spiritual activity. We are born with a strong sense of responsibility and the self-esteem that goes with it. We must continually, through our lives, be responsible and meet each task so that other people can rely upon us. When we accomplish acts that show responsibility, our self-esteem is held in good health. We should learn continually to be responsible for our own belongings, our own health and condition and all other aspects of the building of a purposeful life by being responsible. One of the best ways to acquire self confidence at any age is to tackle a problem, getting proper support and encouragement, having our efforts affirmed and completing the tasks in the best way we know how.

When you are responsible, you keep your agreements, you make sure things get done. When we are a responsible person and we make a mistake, we also take the responsibility for it. Being responsible is one of the most important aspects of the mature person.

When you take responsibility for your own actions, others can count on you. When you are willing to be accountable, you will get a lot of things done, and people will trust you. When something goes right or wrong, people like to know who to thank or who to go to in order to make things right, or correct them. When you act responsibly, people know they can come to you to set things right. When people are not willing to be responsible, things they have agreed to do may never get done. Some people just make excuses instead of taking responsibility for their actions. When we are a responsible person, people depend on us and we can probably depend on them.

I WILL TAKE ON ALL MY NEW RESPONSIBILITIES WITH AN ATTITUDE OF EXCELLENCE. I WILL SHOW RESPONSIBLE BEHAVIOR. I WILL BE A RESPONSIBLE INDIVIDUAL.

Reverence

Reverence is treating everything involving God, religion and worship with deep respect.

Reverence means acting in a very special way. Being reverent is behaving as if you were in the constant presence of God. It doesn't matter whether you are in a place of worship (churches, synagogue, or a building) or riding in your car or walking along a beautiful river. It is always important to be reverent where God is concerned. One should always show reverence in prayer and meditation. One should only speak of God in the highest of respect and reverence.

When your religion has rules for how to act while you are worshiping, reverence is to be careful and respectful in following those rules because you are showing your respect to your Creator. Reverence is a quality of your spirit. It allows you to feel the presence of God. If you didn't treat the experience of worship and the sacred things that go with it with reverence, then these most important things become quite ordinary. All things associated with the worship of God are the most sacred and special things in this world and deserve our most respectful behavior. Some people show no reverence for living things. They treat them carelessly instead of revering them as part of His creation. All of the natural world, all of the seas and oceans, the land, the mountains, the trees and flowers and all animals are His creation, they should also be treated with reverence and respect. One of the most important parts of life is to become still and quiet and listen to your heart and meditation.

When we are reverent, it allows us to feel God's love. Reverence can be experienced in times of prayer, meditation or communion with Him. It is choosing not to think about anything else at that time. You concentrate your whole being on the sacredness of that moment and that act. Reverence allows us to listen when God speaks to our heart. Reverence also means respecting others when they are worshiping Him in their own way, being quiet and not interrupting. Being reverent for all of God's creation is to have an attitude of respect for all living things.

When one shows reverence, by learning how worship is practiced by many people, we naturally become more mature. You must treat all the holy books of different religions as the most special and important things in the world, for in fact, they are.

It is important to develop the obedience of inner stillness so that we may hear when God speaks to our heart. When we are reverent, we recognize the special and sacred things of our world. If we are to become all that we were designed to be, we must become reverent and loving and know the sacredness of the Creator of the universe.

> I WILL BE A REVERENT PERSON, SHOWING RESPECT FOR GOD, RELIGION AND WORSHIP. I WILL TAKE SOME TIME EACH DAY TO BE STILL, TO TURN TO HIM AND TO LISTEN WITH MY HEART AND SPIRIT. I WILL TREAT SACRED THINGS AND ALL OF NATURE WITH REVERENCE.

SELF-DISCIPLINE

Self-discipline is self control.

Self-discipline is bringing order and efficiency into your life. It means getting yourself to do what you really want to do rather than being blown in the wind of your thoughts or feelings. Self-discipline means choosing to do what you feel is right. With self-discipline, you can be moderate. You don't overdo things or let yourself become lazy. You learn to get things done. You may not be able to control your thoughts and feelings but you can control what you do with them. You don't lose control of yourself when you feel hurt or angry, but you decide the best way to solve problems.

When you are self-disciplined, you create structure in your life. The person who is self-disciplined does not procrastinate. They get things done. With self-discipline, you take charge of yourself. It is so important to develop self-discipline. You will then control your own behavior, so others don't have to. Self-discipline brings you freedom. You develop efficiency so you don't have to feel over burdened by all the tasks that are waiting for you. Self-discipline creates a life of accomplishment. Self-discipline avoids procrastination, which can become a heavy burden.

When people do not have self-discipline, they lose control of their emotions. Without self-discipline, life is chaotic. When you are a person maturing in self-discipline, no one has to watch you or control you, because you are watching yourself and exercising self-control.

When a person has self-discipline they can create their own routines. They can plan their days better and have more free time. You put limits on yourself, such as the amount of television you watch. When you have self-discipline you use detachment so your emotions won't control you. You get things done in an orderly and efficient way. When we have self-discipline, we choose to obey the rules.

EVERY ONE MUST DEVELOP SELF-DISCIPLINE. WE MUST USE OUR TIME WELL AND GET THINGS DONE. WE SHOULD CHOOSE OUR ACTIONS WITH DETACHMENT, DETERMINATION AND SELF DISCIPLINE.

SINCERITY

Sincerity means to be genuine, real, honest and without pretense or deceit.

A sincere person is genuine and believes in a purity in what they do and say. We can count on a sincere person being real and true. When we exhibit the virtue of sincerity, we show a heartfelt, wholehearted attitude about what we are doing or saying. We show empathy and feeling for other people. Sincerity means the opposite of hypocrisy, falsifying, or exaggerating. When we are sincere, we are earnest and show devotion without reservation. Sincerity is a virtue from the heart and shows depth of a genuine feeling about something. We express our inner self towards other people in a heartfelt manner.

Without sincerity, we could not trust anyone. If they were not sincere, we would not know if they were falsifying, lying to us, or exaggerating. We must show sincerity for many reasons. It appears at the present time, that the virtue of sincerity is not extended to our society in a comfortable degree. We must all strive to be sincere and induce sincerity in the society around us.

When we are sincere, we are a positive influence to our self and to everyone around us.

We show an enthusiastic, honest display of our feelings and attitudes. We help with the spontaneity and the harmony of the world around us when we are sincere. Sincerity is a most important virtue and brings inner joy and peacefulness to the sincere one and people around us.

> **SINCERITY IS THE ABSENCE OF PRETENSE. WHEN WE ARE SINCERE, WE ARE HONEST AND DO NOT EXAGGERATE OR LIE. WE ARE GENUINE. I WILL IMPROVE MY CHARACTER BY ALWAYS BEING SINCERE.**

SPIRITUALITY

Spirituality is the composite of divine light and virtuous attributes within you.

Spirituality is not a single virtue, it is all the virtues and more. Although mankind has focused on the body, the brain, or the mind in most of its studies, we now know that spirituality is mostly what we are. When we talk about spirituality and being spiritual, we are talking about an attitude toward God and the inner aspects of our soul, our enlightenment within spirituality. When we are spiritual, we are expanding the God-like qualities of love, kindness, compassion, forgiveness, and justice, etc. When we reach for the energizing spirituality of our lives, we can develop a blissful condition within ourselves. Spirituality and the seeking of the spiritual consciousness brings us by its very nature into joyfulness and a happy, progressive life. We will find that healthy energies are part of our spirituality.

The true spiritual understanding of the human condition is just now being brought to the forefront of reality, the knowing of the Godliness within ourselves. When we become spiritually conscious, we will have the eyes to see the vision and the ears to hear the truth of our own spirituality. When we recognize, obey, and act spiritually, the negative aspects of life cannot intrude into our daily behavior. When we become spiritually conscious, we no longer deal with anger, greed, jealousy, spite, lust, fear, anxiety, or turmoil. These negative aspects wastefully take away our energy and undermine our hope in achieving a spiritual, productive, and harmonious life. The lower levels of materialism are a sabotage for your true spiritual essence, the God within all of us.

We must all seek the truth of spirituality, both personal and global. When we become spiritual, we find we have a universal source of energy. We have a natural peacefulness. You find that you are loved and you can love when you become spiritually conscious. When we develop our spirituality, we are keener, more capable, loving, appreciating, and truly successful human beings. It is important to take a moment each day in absolute silence and peace to pray or meditate about your connection with the creator of the universe and your specific purpose. It is important to know that when you try hard to become spiritual, you will become free. You will relieve yourself of the bondage of self. Freedom can only be attained in spiritual hopefulness by letting material idols go.

In this day, we must recognize that the purpose of our highest self is to embrace the fullness of God in all you see and do. Our present conditions of love, joy, harmony, progress, and fulfillment are directly related to our willingness and ability to reach high conscious spiritual levels of understanding and behavior. When you recognize your spiritual greatness, you no longer have enemies to deal with for no one is your enemy. You no longer have prejudice or hatred that divides humanity. You are unable to participate in the negative behaviors. On a mutual basis, you become harmonious and one with all things around you. Friendships become easy to develop because you are a kind and loving spiritual person. One of the greatest gifts of seeking your spiritual consciousness is that you recognize that you are limitless and that everything around you, everything you desire or plan to do can become a reality.

YOUR SPIRITUALITY IS THE REAL YOU. WHEN WE GROW IN SPIRITUAL CONSCIOUSNESS, WE CAN FIND SOLUTIONS TO ALL PROBLEMS. HUMBLE SPIRITUALITY REDUCES EGO DRIVEN BEHAVIOR. I WILL STRIVE DAILY TO BECOME A SPIRITUALLY CONSCIOUS, KNOWLEDGEABLE PERSON. VIRTUES ARE THE INDIVIDUAL BUILDING BLOCKS OF SPIRITUALITY OR GOD-LIKE ATTRIBUTES OF OUR VERY BEING.

- *Study your virtues, they become your success path.*

- *Virtues make us truly great!*

- *Learn to think of others before yourself; you will grow.*

- *It is not what you do so much as what you are.*

STEADFASTNESS

Steadfastness is being steady & dependable no matter what.

We can accomplish any project to it's very end if we keep on going, not if we hang in there. Steadfastness is being faithful and purposeful. Steadfastness if remaining true to someone or something in spite of any test or obstacles that appear to stop you. When you are steadfast, you commit yourself to something for however long it takes.

Steadfastness is actually harder than faithfulness and purposefulness. It means you know what you are getting into and have all the commitment you need. You never stop or waiver because you care so much about your commitment.

When we lack steadfastness, we can be enthusiastic and committed one minute and doubtful the next. We must finish something we have agreed to do. It is important for people to be able to count on you. If you are not steadfast, you can just stop any time - without any feelings about what has actually happened.

When we are steadfast, we can handle our doubts because we know we can complete any project. We know where we stand for the long run. Other people are reassured by the strength and dependability of our commitments. With steadfastness, we find ourselves at peace in the face of doubt or trouble. When we develop the virtue of steadfastness, we remain steady, keeping the same pace. When we are doing a job, we should keep at it without going too fast to tire ourselves or too slow to get it done on time.

It is important to be steadfast in a relationship. You stick by the person even when they aren't much fun or they need a lot of attention or they are going through hard times. When we are reliable and steadfast, we stay unwavering in our commitment to see things through.

I WILL BE A STEADFAST PERSON. I WILL BE STEADY IN WHAT I CHOOSE TO DO. I WILL BE STEADFAST AND NEVER GIVE UP. I WILL BE A LOYAL AND COMMITTED FRIEND.

Tactfulness

Tactfulness is telling the truth in a way that no one is disturbed or offended.

It has been written, "A soft answer turneth away wrath." Tactfulness is knowing what to say and what is better left unsaid. Tactfulness is showing another person the truth in a way that makes it very easy for them to hear and accept it. Tactfulness is a very mature way of acting and a wonderful virtue.

Often, in a fit of anger or hurt, we say things in a way that we should not. Rather than tell a lie, being tactful means that you look for a way to share the truth so that it helps rather than hurts other people. When we are angry or upset, we should stop, think, and become tactful.

Tactfulness is also very important in knowing when to stay silent. It is sometimes keeping things to yourself unless there is a really good reason to speak. When asked a direct question, we should always reply, but with tactfulness. One of the most important aspects of being tactful is that we do not point out people's differences or mistakes to embarrass them. We must be careful about other's feelings as you would like them to be of yours.

When we are not tactful, we can be rude and blunt. We should not go around saying whatever pops into our head. When we are not tactful, we can be insensitive to others. Insensitive people may tell the truth, but they do it in a way which is painful to others. When people are angry, they say things which can damage a relationship unless they are tactful. When we are being tactful, the truth is always told with gentleness and kindness. Other people will listen to us so that problems can be worked out if we do it with tactfulness. We all grow and learn when the truth is presented to us with tact. The key to tactfulness is to think before you speak. Being tactful is a sign of empathy and kindness.

We must learn to stop and think before we speak. You must decide whether to keep quiet or speak up. We should be tactful by keeping things to ourselves if telling others might hurt them. If we must speak up, let us do it in a sensitive way concerning other's feelings. Don't do it in front of other people or in a way that will embarrass them. Rather than just attacking someone with your words, wait until you can calmly tell them what is bothering you in an objective and kindly manner.

I WILL BE A TACTFUL PERSON. I WILL THINK BEFORE I SPEAK AND BE SENSITIVE TO OTHER PEOPLE'S FEELINGS AND CONDITIONS. BEING TACTFUL IS COMPLYING WITH THE GOLDEN RULE, "DO UNTO OTHERS AS YOU WOULD HAVE THEM DO UNTO YOU."

- *O' my friend, in the garden of your heart plant the rose of love and understanding.*

- *You are a chosen person, live up to it.*

- *Be glad for life, it will treat you well.*

- *Be glad for life, God gave it to you!*

TOLERANCE

Tolerance is being able to accept things that you wish were different.

Some people find it difficult to tolerate any change in the way they want things to be. They fuss and fume if it's too hot or cold, too noisy or too quiet, or if something is taking too long, they become impatient. If you are a tolerant person and someone annoys you, you just go on and don't pay too much attention. When you are a tolerant person, you accept things you don't like about people. You recognize that they have a right to be themselves even though they might be quite different from you. You learn to tolerate because of the love that you have for other human beings. Deep down we all care about each other.

When you are tolerant, you are able to sort out what is important from what is not. You show patience and forgiveness when people make mistakes. You accept what you cannot change with grace and dignity.

There are many signs to watch for in people who are intolerant. These people cannot stand to have anything differ from what they want or expect. They tend to criticize, complain, and condemn people for doing things they don't like. They try to change other people, rather than understanding them or overlooking their faults. They have difficulty forgiving.

Without tolerance, people are unhappy most of the time. When we are developing tolerance, there is a space to be and space to grow. If there is something we don't like about each other, we overlook it out of love or friendship. This gives us all an opportunity to work on ourselves because we want to and not because we have to. When we are tolerant, we don't allow differences to drive us apart. We recognize the wonderful similarity and simple needs of all of our fellow human beings. We should not expect others to be just like us. As we mature, we find out that differences are not a defect, just wonderful differences. Being tolerant allows the give and take in a relationship so that it may grow and prosper. Tolerance is a soft, kindly virtue of understanding that gives you the strength to recognize when to stand up for your rights.

I WILL BE A TOLERANT PERSON. I WILL OVERLOOK PEOPLE'S FAULTS, KNOWING I HAVE A FEW OF MY OWN. I WILL BE OPEN TO DIFFERENCES AND RESPECT THEM. GOD, HELP ME TO ACCEPT THE THINGS I CANNOT CHANGE, MAKE ME A TOLERANT PERSON.

- *Forever is beating at the doors of your soul; let God in!*

- *Be glad for your life, show kindness of heart, gentleness of manner and love to all.*

- *No person can live without God! Otherwise they will choose a false God that will delude and betray them.*

- *Life is for living, not existing.*

Trust

Trust is believing in or relying on someone or something without having control.

We all trust the sun to rise in the morning without having to do a single thing. Trust in God is essential to life. He created you because He loved you. We trust people like our parents, grandparents, teachers, some friends, and authorities to do what they say they are going to do without having to make them do it. People who want to be worthy of your trust are those who really try to make what they do and what they say match exactly. This is how trust is built.

Without trust, you always feel like you have to control things to make them turn out right. Even things that you cannot control start to worry you. Trust leaves you free to concentrate on those things that you need to do. You do not waste energy worrying about the things that other people are doing when you trust them.

To develop trust, one must have a basic confidence that things will go right. Trust the rightness of things until you have lots of reasons to think that things are going wrong. It is important to remember that when things are difficult or are going wrong, we can always trust in God. When we develop a trusting nature, we grow stronger and we learn new things because we trust. Trust allows us to relax about things turning out all right. Instead of spending the energy to worry, you let your fears come and go.

If a person fails your trust, give them a chance to explain and really listen to what they have to say. If their explanation makes sense to you, then tell them you understand and start over. But if we find some people keep repeating this distrust, then we probably must tell them we cannot trust you. You will start trusting them when they decide to become trustworthy.

> I TRUST GOD THAT EVERYTHING WHICH HAPPENS TODAY IS FOR MY GOOD. I WILL NOT WORRY OR TRY TO CONTROL OTHERS. I WILL TRUST OTHERS TO KEEP THEIR PROMISES.

TRUSTWORTHINESS

Trustworthiness means being worthy of trust.

When you are trustworthy, if you make a promise or a vow you keep your word no matter how hard it becomes. Trustworthiness means you can be counted on. When we are trustworthy and people give us things for safe keeping, they know there is a sacred trust and things will be safe. When we are trustworthy, people can give us money to keep for them, documents, possessions of many different kinds, and they know they are safe. Being trustworthy means that if someone asked you to do something and you start out to do it, you will finish it.

People who are trustworthy are known for their determination, their reliability, and their truthfulness. They keep their word. When we are not trustworthy, agreements and promises don't mean much. When people are not trustworthy, sometimes they keep a promise and sometimes they don't. You never know what you can expect of someone who is untrustworthy. When someone cannot be trusted, people become sad and disappointed. If we are not trustworthy, people never know if they can believe you or count on you.

When we are trustworthy, other people don't have to doubt you or check up on you to see if you are doing something you promised to do.

You develop trustworthiness by making a promise to someone. Decide to keep your promise rather than just trying to. Start doing what you agreed to do and watch out for things which could prevent you from keeping your agreement. There are obstacles that come along, like distractions or not feeling like doing it, or a job being much harder than you thought it would be. It is important in developing trustworthiness that you stop and think before making a promise. Be sure it is something you really want to do and that you really can do.

When you are trustworthy, you keep your word. It is very important to you to be worthy of the trust of others. When people are trustworthy, they can be trusted to tell the truth, to do their part, to give their best. A trustworthy person is the best friend anyone could ever have.

I WILL BE A TRUSTWORTHY PERSON. I WILL KEEP MY PROMISES AND BE WORTHY OF THE TRUST OTHERS PLACE IN.

TRUTHFULNESS

Truthfulness means your words and actions are full of truth.

Telling the truth means you don't tell lies, even to protect yourself or anyone else. You don't live a lie either. You show people you love, who and what you are without exaggerating to impress them or trying to look like something you are not. When you are developing truthfulness, you don't try to believe something you know isn't true. You don't lie to others and you don't lie to yourself.

Truthfulness is knowing the difference between what is real and what is fantasy. You can have them both for fantasy is acceptable fun, but you do not mix them up if you are being truthful.

When we lack truthfulness, no one can tell if there is a lie or a truth before us. People who cannot be trusted to tell the difference between what is true or what is false, cannot tell which is fact or fiction. Without trust, there is confusion and disunity.

We are living in truthfulness when what we say can be trusted. We should say what we mean and mean what we say. Truthfulness builds bonds of love and trust. People know where they stand with an honest and truthful person. When we investigate the truth for ourselves, we don't allow others to dictate their thinking or meaning. A truthful person does not form prejudices or come to unfair or untrue conclusions. Truthful people believe in justice and truth.

When you develop truthfulness, you choose to tell the truth no matter what. If someone asks you what you think, you tell them what you really think, but tactfully. To develop truthfulness by using justice and discernment recognizing what is true from what is false and discerning what you want to say. If people try to tell you something about another person and you have not seen it with your own eyes, you don't accept it as truth. You investigate the truth for yourself. With discernment you can tell the difference between fantasy and reality. We should not mix them up. If you want to use your imagination, great! It is one of God's gifts.

A truthful person, doesn't exaggerate to look more important. You are already quite important enough!

> I WILL BE A TRUTHFUL PERSON. I WILL INVESTIGATE THE TRUTH FOR MYSELF. I HAVE NO NEED TO IMPRESS OTHERS OR EXAGGERATE. I CAN FACE THE TRUTH AND BE TRUSTED TO SPEAK THE TRUTH.

UNDERSTANDING

Understanding is knowing and caring, being sympathetic and tolerant.

In the creation of human kind, God gave us many special gifts. Four of the main gifts are the ability to grow and develop in wisdom, knowledge, understanding, and discernment. We should all strive to understand and develop these gifts that have been bestowed upon God's special creation - human kind. Understanding is the process of comprehending and knowing about things. We are able to know about the world and the people who live on it by being understanding. When we are understanding, we are given the power of comprehension and knowing. It is important in all studies to dedicate ourselves to understanding their true meaning.

When we are understanding, we recognize other people's conditions and problems and we show sympathy. When we have understanding, we have a tolerant attitude towards people and events. Understanding is a very important tool of life and is among the most important virtues. It gives us the ability to learn and to study and to understand what we are trying to do or what we are trying to learn. Understanding is the wonderful gift that allows us to learn.

One of the highest qualities that one can achieve is to be mature in understanding. It gives us the power of discernment, of insight to interpret other people's feelings and conditions accurately and to comprehend relationships and the particulars involved. It is so important to be understanding in order to develop friendly or harmonious relationships. When we are understanding, we will find agreement of opinion or feelings easy to achieve. We can make the adjustments of differences and proceed in a joyful manner. When we are understanding, we will strive for mutual agreements.

The importance of understanding is that it brings knowledge and increases our intelligence. When we are endowed with understanding, we will become tolerant and sympathetic which will develop harmonies in our lives instead of conflict. If the world would become more understanding, it would by that very nature become more peaceful and harmonious.

> WE SHOULD ALWAYS REMEMBER THAT UNDERSTANDING AND DISCERNMENT BRINGS ABOUT WISDOM AND KNOWLEDGE. I WILL STRIVE TO BE MORE UNDERSTANDING OF OTHER PEOPLE. I WILL DILIGENTLY TRY TO EXCEL IN NOT ONLY MY LEARNING PROCESS, BUT I WILL BE KIND, COURTEOUS, AND UNDERSTANDING.

Personal Virtues Score Card
Beginning audit

Score Virtues from 1-10

Assertiveness _____
Care _____
Character _____
Class _____
Cleanliness _____
Compassion _____
Confidence _____
Consideration _____
Cooperation _____
Courage _____
Courtesy _____
Creativity _____
Detachment _____
Determination _____
Discernment _____
Empathy _____
Enthusiasm _____
Excellence _____
Faithfulness _____
Flexibility _____
Forgiveness _____
Friendliness _____
Generosity _____
Gentleness _____
Giving _____
Goodness _____
Gratitude _____
Helpfulness _____

Honesty _____
Honorableness _____
Humility _____
Idealism _____
Integrity _____
Joyfulness _____
Justice _____
Kindness _____
Love _____
Loyalty _____
Mercy _____
Moderation _____
Modesty _____
Obedience _____
Orderliness _____
Patience _____
Peacefulness _____
Prayerfulness _____
Purpose _____
Reliability _____
Respect _____
Responsibility _____
Reverence _____
Self-Discipline _____
Sincerity _____
Spirituality _____
Steadfastness _____
Tactfulness _____
Tolerance _____
Trust _____
Trustworthiness _____
Truthfulness _____
Understanding _____

Personal Virtues Score Card
Beginning Audit
Score Virtues from 1-10

Assertiviness _____
Care _____
Character _____
Class _____
Cleanliness _____
Compassion _____
Confidence _____
Consideration _____
Cooperation _____
Courage _____
Courtesy _____
Creativity _____
Det _____
Determination _____
Discernment _____
Empathy _____
Enthusiasm _____
Excellence _____
Faithfulness _____
Flexibility _____
Forgiveness _____
Friendliness _____
Generosity _____
Gentleness _____
Giving _____
Goodness _____
Gratitude _____
Helpfulness _____

Honesty _____
Honorableness _____
Humility _____
Idealism _____
Integrity _____
Joyfulness _____
Justice _____
Kindness _____
Love _____
Loyalty _____
Mercy _____
Moderation _____
Modesty _____
Obedience _____
Orderliness _____
Patience _____
Peacefulness _____
Prayerfulness _____
Purpose _____
Reliability _____
Respect _____
Responsibility _____
Reverence _____
Self-Discipline _____
Sincerity _____
Spirituality _____
Steadfastness _____
Tactfulness _____
Tolerance _____
Trust _____
Trustworthiness _____
Truthfulness _____
Understanding _____

**GO
IN
LOVE
AND
PEACE !**

IN THE GREATNESS OF THE HUMAN IS THE MAGNIFICENT GIFTS OF WILL AND CHOICE.

Keep your <u>will</u> strong and use this knowledge learned to make the right choices for yourself and all you survey.

Thank you, Don Decker